MW00491420

SAN JUAN & PUERTO RICO'S EAST COAST

SUZANNE VAN ATTEN

Contents

SAN JUAN & PUERTO RICO'S EAST COAST

SAN JUAN

San Juan, Puerto Rico, is arguably the most cosmopolitan city in the Caribbean. The second-oldest European settlement in the Americas, it is a place where world-class restaurants and luxury hotels compete for space alongside glitzy nightclubs and casinos; where Spanish colonial and neoclassical buildings line cobblestone streets; where designer stores and import shops beckon spend-happy tourists; where art, music, and dance thrive in its theaters, museums, and festivals; and where you're never very far from wide strips of sand and surf, ideal for sailing, sunbathing, and swimming.

Situated on the northeastern coast of Puerto Rico, San Juan stretches along 25 miles of coastline and 10 miles inland. It spans 30,000 acres of coastal plain, encompassing rivers, bays, and lagoons, and is home to 1.1 million residents in the greater San Juan area. Established by Spain as the island's capital in 1521, the city's early role as a military stronghold is evident in its 16th- and 17th-century fortresses and a nearly 400-year-old city wall erected around the oldest part of the city to protect it from foreign attacks.

The heart of the city is historic Old San Juan, a 45-block grid of blue cobblestone streets lined with pastel 16th–18th-century buildings trimmed with ornamental ironwork and hanging balconies. By day its streets crawl with tourists shopping for souvenirs and designer duds. At night it throbs with locals and tourists alike, both partaking of some of the city's finest restaurants and nightclubs.

But Old San Juan is only the tip of the city. Travel eastward along the coast to Condado,

considered the city's tourist district. High-rise hotels, condos, and apartment buildings overlook the Atlantic Ocean. High-end shops line the main thoroughfare, Avenida Ashford, and many fine restaurants and casinos serve night crawlers.

Continue eastward to Ocean Park, a gated residential community on a fine beach with a handful of guesthouses and restaurants. Beside it is Isla Verde, where the city's best beaches and most exclusive hotels are, along with fast-food restaurants and a cockfight arena.

Though it may seem so, San Juan isn't all beachfront property. Travel inland for a locals-only experience in Hato Ray, San Juan's commercial district; Río Piedras, home of the University of Puerto Rico; and Bayamón, a bedroom community.

As in any large city, all is not paradise. San Juan is a densely populated metropolis thick with automobile traffic. A heavy cruise-ship trade dumps thousands of tourists in the city several days a week, and the number of trinket shops catering to day-trippers has proliferated. Burger Kings and Pizza Huts are not an uncommon sight. Neither are pockets of poor neighborhoods, some of whose residents contribute to a petty street-crime problem.

But despite its big-city ways, San Juan's natural beauty is apparent in its miles of sandy beaches, its shady plazas, and its beloved *coqui,* a tiny tree frog whose "co-QUI" song fills the air. As it's a commonwealth of the United States, American influence is clearly present, but San Juan proudly maintains its Spanish heritage in its language, its culture, and its customs. And although its future is firmly planted in the 21st century, San Juan's rich history endures in its carefully preserved architecture, its stately fortresses, and the hearts of its inhabitants.

PLANNING YOUR TIME

It's possible to hit San Juan's highlights in a single long weekend, but it's equally possible to spend a whole month here and not see all the city has to offer.

Six municipalities make up greater San Juan.

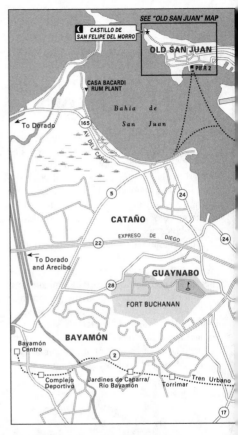

They include San Juan, Cataño, Bayamón, Guaynabo, Trujillo Alto, and Carolina. The four sectors that visitors gravitate to are Old San Juan, Condado, Ocean Park, and Isla Verde in the municipalities of San Juan and Carolina. Not surprisingly, all four areas are along the coast, and luckily they are within about 20 minutes of one another by car or taxi. Most are also accessible by bus.

Old San Juan

Old San Juan is the cultural center of Puerto Rico. The 500-year-old city is filled with many historic buildings, Spanish forts, museums, restaurants, bars, shops, and ship docks. Beach access is very limited in Old San Juan, and a

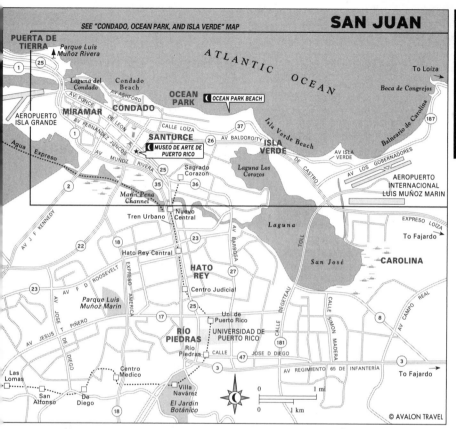

thick concentration of tourists can be found here, especially on days the cruise ships dock. But its charm is undeniable.

Among Old San Juan's many must-see sites are the city's two Spanish fortresses, **Castillo de San Felipe del Morro** and **Castillo de San Cristóbal;** the significant religious sites of **Catedral de San Juan Bautista** and **Capilla del Cristo;** and two terrific museums, Museo de Las Americas and La Casa de Libro.

The best way to see Old San Juan is by foot. The roads are drivable, but they're narrow and one-way, and only residents' automobiles are permitted in at night. If walking gets to be too much, there is a free trolley service that runs through the southern half of the city where most of the shops

are. Navigation in and out of Old San Juan is easy. The main public bus terminal is near the cruise-ship piers on Calle de Marina, just below Plaza de Colón in Old San Juan, and there are taxi stands in front of most plazas and hotels.

Condado and Miramar

Condado is considered San Juan's tourist district, although Old San Juan and Isla Verde could qualify for the same designation. The community, which runs along a stretch of beach between Old San Juan and Isla Verde, is undergoing a dramatic transformation. Once the height of glamour, this strip of flashy resorts and hotels fell onto hard times during the recession of the early 1980s, and many hotels closed.

HIGHLIGHTS

◖ Ocean Park Beach: Easy access and pristine sand make Ocean Park Beach an excellent place to spend the day in the sun. Due to its central location, it's a short cab ride from anywhere in the city. On weekends, lounge chairs are available for rent and street vendors patrol the area selling snacks and beverages (page 14).

◖ Castillo de San Felipe del Morro: Established in 1539, this imposing Spanish colonial fortress was designed so sentries could spot enemies entering San Juan Bay. That's what makes it such an exceptional place to admire the views. The vast lawn is a great spot to fly a kite too (page 14).

◖ Castillo de San Cristóbal: Built to protect San Juan from attack by land, San Cristóbal was begun in 1634 and eventually encompassed 27 acres, making it the largest fort on the island. It provides an excellent vantage point for checking out stunning views of the city (page 14).

◖ Museo de Arte de Puerto Rico: This impressive new 130,000-square-foot museum showcases Puerto Rican art from the 17th century to the present, from classical portraiture to politically charged conceptual art. As an added bonus, the wall text is in Spanish and English (page 19).

◖ Catedral de San Juan Bautista: Established in 1521, the cathedral lays claim to being the oldest existing church in the Western Hemisphere. The current structure dates from the 1800s or early 1900s and contains the tomb of Juan Ponce de León (page 20).

◖ Nuyorican Café: The casual Old San Juan nightclub is the hot spot for live salsa music every night but Monday. This is where locals go to dance the night away on the tiny dance floor. Get there early if you want a seat (page 27).

LOOK FOR ◖ TO FIND RECOMMENDED SIGHTS, ACTIVITIES, DINING, AND LODGING.

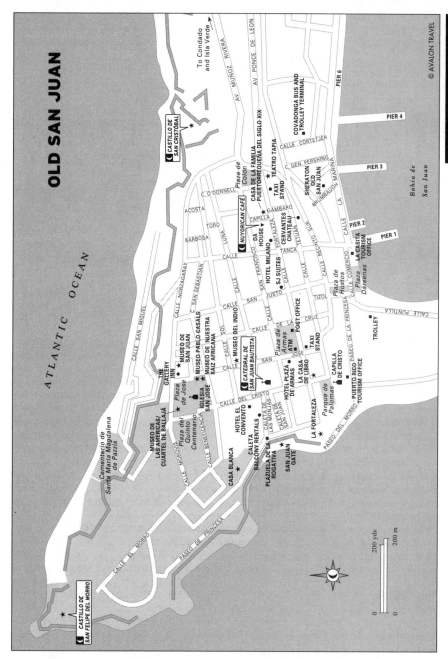

OLD SAN JUAN

ATLANTIC OCEAN

To Condado
and Isla Verde

© AVALON TRAVEL

CASTILLO DE
SAN CRISTÓBAL

AV. MUÑOZ RIVERA

AV. PONCE DE LEON

PIER 6

PIER 4

CALLE CORTETJER

C. GEN PERSHING   PIER 3

Bahía de
San Juan

COVADONGA BUS AND
TROLLEY TERMINAL

TEATRO TAPIA

SHERATON
OLD
SAN JUAN

BRUMBAUGH MARINA

LA PUNTILLA

Plaza de
Colón

CASA DE LA FAMILIA
PUERTORREQUEÑA DEL SIGLO XIX

TAXI
STAND

CALLE CORTETJER

GÁMBARO

CAPILLA

NUYORICAN CAFÉ

C. O'DONNELL

ACOSTA

TORO

BARBOSA

CALLE

LUNA

CALLE SAN SEBASTIÁN

CALLE NORZAGARAY

CALLE SAN MIGUEL

Cementerio de
Santa María Magdalena
de Pazzis

MUSEO DE
LAS AMÉRICAS/
CUARTEL DE BALLAJÁ

CALLE MORIVIS

Plaza del
Quinto
Centenario

CALLE BENEFICENCIA

CASA BLANCA

CALETA
BALCONY RENTALS

PLAZUELA DE LA
ROGATIVA

SAN JUAN
GATE

CALLE EL MORRO

PASEO DE PRINCESA

CASTILLO DE
SAN FELIPE DEL MORRO

CALLE SAN JUSTO

CALLE SAN FRANCISCO

CALLE DE LA CRUZ

CALLE FORTALEZA

CALLE TETUÁN

CALLE TANCA

CALLE RECINTO SUR

CALLE COMERCIO

PIER 2

PIER 1

LA CASITA
TOURISM
OFFICE

CERVANTES
CHATEAU

HOTEL MILANO

SJ SUITES

Plaza de
Hostos

Plaza
Dársenas

TROLLEY

Plaza de
Armas

POST OFFICE

ATM

TAXI
STAND

LA CASA
DEL LIBRO

CAPILLA
DE CRISTO

PUERTO RICO
TOURISM OFFICE

PASEO DE LA PRINCESA

PASEO DEL MORRO

LA FORTALEZA

Parque de
Palomas

HOTEL PLAZ

CATEDRAL DE
SAN JUAN BAUTISTA

CALLE DEL CRISTO

HOTEL EL
CONVENTO

IGLESIA
SAN JOSÉ

Plaza
de José

THE
GALLERY
INN

MUSEO DE
SAN JUAN

MUSEO PABLO CASALS

MUSEO DE NUESTRA
RAÍZ AFRICANA

MUSEO DEL INDIO

CALLE SOL

CALLE DE LAS MONJAS

CALLE SAN JOSÉ

CALLE SAN

CALETA
DE LAS MONJAS

CALETA
SAN JUAN

TIZOL

200 yds

200 m

0

0

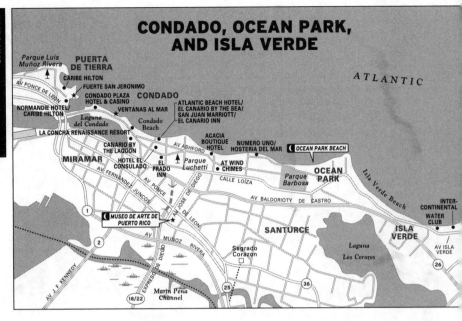

But things are on the upswing. Several cranes hang over Avenida Ashford as old buildings are undergoing renovation and new construction is under way. New parks have blossomed, giving passersby access to the Atlantic Ocean and a great place to relax and people-watch.

Aside from its beaches and hotels, Condado is home to some excellent restaurants and casinos, and it is the best place to go for upscale shopping at places such as Louis Vuitton and Cartier. Taxis and public buses traverse the area frequently, and its wide sidewalks and browse-friendly businesses make it an excellent place for pedestrians.

Miramar, an upscale residential area overlooking Laguna del Condado, has recently been designated a historic district and is scheduled for millions of dollars in improvements.

Isla Verde

Isla Verde is renowned for its long, wide beaches, its luxury resorts, and some pretty spectacular nightclubs and casinos. When you're catching some rays on the beach or partying the night away in a glitzy hot spot, it can feel as glamorous as a mini–South Beach. Unfortunately, the only way to actually see Isla Verde's gorgeous coast is from one of the high-rise hotels and condominiums that line every inch of the way. And the traffic-choked main thoroughfare, Avenida Isla Verde, is a jumble of fast-food restaurants, pizzerias, souvenir shops, tattoo parlors, condom shops, and so on. The community is also home to the Aeropuerto Internacional Luis Muñoz Marín.

The best way to enjoy Isla Verde is to ensconce oneself in one of the community's cushy seaside resorts and stay there.

Ocean Park and Santurce

Wedged between Condado and Isla Verde is a tiny oasis of quiet gentility called Ocean Park. Primarily a gated residential neighborhood, the ocean-side community has only a handful of restaurants, and shopping is nonexistent. But there are several very nice guesthouses right on the beach, and they're excellent places to stay if you want a refuge from busy urban settings and crowded tourist attractions. There's also

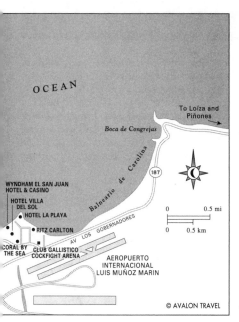

an excellent stretch of well-maintained public beach with parking.

Just a few blocks inland from Condado is Santurce, a congested conglomeration of small shops and businesses that cater to residents of the island. Tourists are advised to take precautions when visiting the area at night as it has a high rate of street crime. Nevertheless, it is home to the superb **Museo de Arte de Puerto Rico** and several popular nightclubs.

Hato Rey, Río Piedras, and Bayamón

Outside San Juan's popular tourist areas are communities central to the lives of San Juan residents. Hato Rey is the city's business and financial district, chock-full of banks and restaurants that cater to businessmen and women. It's connected by the new 10-mile Tren Urbano metro system to Río Piedras, home of the University of Puerto Rico and El Jardín Botánico, and the residential area of Bayamón, home of Parque de las Ciencias Luis A. Ferre science park.

Several spectacular day trips are less than an hour's drive east of San Juan, the most popular being **El Yunque Caribbean National Forest,** the rain forest, and **Balneario La Monserrate,** considered one of Puerto Rico's most beautiful beaches.

HISTORY

Christopher Columbus was on his second voyage in his quest to "discover" the New World when he arrived in Puerto Rico in 1493. He christened the island San Juan Bautista after John the Baptist, claimed it as a property of Spain, and went on his merry way. But among his crew was a lieutenant named Juan Ponce de León, who shared Columbus's passion for exploration and colonization. In 1508 Ponce de León returned to the island to establish a settlement in a nearly landlocked bit of marshland just west of San Juan, which he called Caparra. He couldn't have made a poorer choice for a new settlement. Virtually uninhabitable and strategically ineffective, the settlement was relocated around 1521 to what is now Old San Juan. Originally the new settlement was called Puerto Rico for its "rich port." It's not clear why—possibly a cartographer's mistake—but soon after it was founded, the name of the settlement was switched with the name of the island.

Sights

BEACHES

Isla Verde Beach (along Ave. Isla Verde) is one of San Juan's most stellar beaches. Roughly two miles long, its wide stretches of sand and rolling surf make for great swimming, surfing, and windsurfing. Like all beaches in Puerto Rico, Isla Verde Beach is open to the public, but because it's lined cheek by jowl with high-rise hotels and apartment buildings, access is limited to narrow walkways between buildings and the occasional dead-end street. Compounding the access problem is the dearth of parking, except for a multilevel lot on the far eastern end.

Condado Beach (along Ave. Ashford) is a less picture-perfect beach than Isla Verde Beach. The terrain is hillier, the sand coarser, and the water less crystalline. But it's got sand, surf, and sun, so it's still got a lot to offer. Like Isla Verde Beach, it's lined with high-rises, but it's much more easily accessible to the general public.

Balneario de Carolina (Carr. 187, Ave. Boca de Congrejas, 787/778-8811, $2) is a public beach maintained by the municipality of Carolina. There are picnic shelters, bathroom facilities, and plenty of parking.

Balneario Escambrón (Carr. 25 in Puerta de Tierra) is the closest beach to Old San Juan. It is a small strip of sand but there's plenty of parking, food vendors, a children's playground, and lifeguards on duty until 5 P.M. Shady characters are known to loiter here after dark.

◖ Ocean Park Beach

Ocean Park Beach is a terrific little residential beach that benefits from ample free parking at Parque Barbosa at the end of Calle McLeary. Due to its central location, it's a short cab ride from anywhere in the city. The section of the beach across from the park is cleaned and raked daily, and a swimming area is marked off with nets to keep out sea creatures. The only drawback is that this part of the beach gets very crowded on weekends and holidays. On weekends, lounge chairs are available for rent, and street vendors patrol the area selling snacks and beverages. Farther east the wind and surf are a little rougher, which makes it popular with sailboarders and kite-surfers. The area in front of the guesthouses inside the gated community of Ocean Park is a popular gay beach.

HISTORIC SIGHTS
◖ Castillo de San Felipe del Morro

It doesn't matter from which direction you approach El Morro (501 Calle Norzagaray, Old San Juan, 787/729-6777, daily 9 A.M.–6 P.M. Dec.–May, daily 9 A.M.–5 P.M. June–Nov., $3 adults, $5 for both forts, $2 seniors over 62, free for children under 16, English tours at 11 A.M. and 3 P.M.), it's an impressive sight to behold. From San Juan Bay, which it was constructed to protect from attack, it's an awesome feat of engineering and a daunting display of military defense featuring four levels of cannon-bearing batteries that rise 140 feet from the sea. From Old San Juan, the approach is more welcoming, thanks to an enormous expanse of grassy lawn and breathtaking views of the shore. It's easy to see why this is such a popular spot for kite-flyers.

Inside El Morro is a maze of rooms, including gun rooms, soldiers' quarters, a chapel, turreted sentry posts, and a prison connected by tunnels, ramps, and a spiral stairway. The foundations for El Morro were laid in 1539, but it wasn't completed until 1787. It successfully endured many foreign attacks by the English in 1595, 1598, and 1797, and by the Dutch in 1625. During the Spanish-American War, the United States fired on El Morro and destroyed the lighthouse, which was later rebuilt.

◖ Castillo de San Cristóbal

San Cristóbal (Calle Norzagaray at the

© SUZANNE VAN ATTEN

Castillo de San Cristóbal

Old San Juan

The recently renovated **Casa Blanca** (1 Calle San Sebastían, Old San Juan, 787/725-1454, Tues.–Sat. 9 A.M.–noon and 1–4 P.M., $2) was originally built as a home for the island's first governor, Juan Ponce de León, although he died on his quest for the Fountain of Youth before he could ever take up residence. Construction was begun in 1523, and for more than 200 years it served as the residence of Ponce de León's descendants. Today it's a museum of 17th- and 18th-century domestic life featuring lots of impressive Spanish antiques. Don't miss the cool, lush gardens that surround the house and the views of both San Juan Bay and the Atlantic Ocean.

La Fortaleza (Calle Fortaleza, Old San Juan, 787/721-7000, ext. 2211, 2323, and 2358, Mon.–Fri. 9 A.M.–3:30 P.M., free) was the first fort built in Puerto Rico, completed in 1540 to provide refuge for the island's original Spanish settlers. Partially burned by the Dutch in 1625, it was rebuilt in the 1640s and received a new facade in 1846. It has been the official residence of the governor of Puerto Rico since the 16th century, which gives it the distinction of the longest continuous use of an executive mansion in the western hemisphere. Tours are limited mostly to the lovely gardens and first floor, with audio narration in Spanish and English.

entrance to Old San Juan, 787/729-6777, daily 9 A.M.–6 P.M. Dec.–May, daily 9 A.M.–5 P.M. June–Nov., $3 adults, $5 for both forts, $2 seniors over 62, free for children under 16, English tours at 10 A.M. and 2 P.M.) is the large fortress at the entrance to Old San Juan by Plaza de Colón. Before it was built, two significant attacks from land—first by the Earl of Cumberland in 1598, later by the Dutch in 1625—convinced the Spanish that protecting the walled city from attack by sea alone was not adequate.

The fort's construction began in 1634 and was completed in 1783. The fort eventually encompassed 27 acres of land, although some of it was destroyed to accommodate the expanding city. The fort's defense was tested in 1797 by another unsuccessful attack by the British. After the United States won the Spanish-American War, it took control of the fort and used it as a World War II observation post. Today, a section of the fort is open to the public, who can wander freely among its intriguing array of tunnels, ramps, stairways, batteries, magazines, soldiers' quarters, and turreted sentry posts.

Aside from El Morro and San Cristóbal's iconic turreted sentry boxes, the most distinguishing characteristic of Old San Juan is **La Muralla,** the grand, dramatic, and impenetrable wall that once surrounded the city and still stands strong along the coast and bay. Nearly 400 years old, the wall took 200 years to complete and stands 48 feet high in some places and 20 feet thick at its base. The wall once had five gates that permitted access into the city, but only one remains today. The commanding red **La Puerta de San Juan** was built in the late 1700s and is on the eastern end of Old San Juan beside La Fortaleza. Sixteen feet tall and 20 feet thick, the door is best seen from the wide bayside promenade,

LA MURALLA

The most enduring symbol of Puerto Rico is La Muralla. Nearly 400 years old, the city wall is composed of rock, rubble, and mortar that wraps around Old San Juan from the cruise-ship piers on San Juan Harbor to the capitol on the Atlantic Ocean. Its iconic sentry boxes serve as a symbol of the island's Spanish heritage and resilience in an ever-changing world.

Begun by Spanish colonists in the 1600s, the wall took 200 years to complete and has withstood multiple attacks by the English, the Dutch, and the Americans. But what proved nearly impenetrable to foreign attack has been rendered defenseless by modern life. Automobile traffic, pollution, and misguided attempts to preserve it have endangered the wall.

Forty-five feet wide and 40 feet high in some spots, La Muralla is crumbling in places. In 2004 a 70-foot section below the heavily traveled Calle Norzagaray fell, underscoring the urgency of stepping up preservation efforts. It wasn't the first time the wall's fragility was made apparent. A larger section fell into San Juan Bay in 1938, and in 1999, a Soviet oil tanker ran aground, damaging the wall's northwest corner.

When the U.S. Army seized Puerto Rico in 1898, it took over maintenance of the wall and attempted its first preservation efforts. Concrete was used to patch La Muralla, but that only served to add weight to the wall and trap moisture inside it, which weakened the structure through time.

Now a National Historic Site, La Muralla is maintained by the National Park Service, which has been overseeing efforts to repair the wall. Experts have spent years studying the 16th-century methods used to build the structure in an attempt to recreate the magic mixture of sand, water, and limestone used to stucco the wall. Not only is the repair method they've developed more effective than concrete, it serves to preserve the wall's historic integrity. The process is now being used to repair the wall's beloved sentry boxes. But it's a painstaking and costly process, requiring the services of specially trained masons, which the Park Service is hard-pressed to fund for large-scale repairs.

But La Muralla endures. Along with the fortresses El Morro and San Cristóbal that adjoin it, the wall attracts 1.2 million visitors a year. Chances are, with the help of preservation efforts, it will continue to assert its soaring beauty and cultural significance as the proud protector of Old San Juan for years to come.

Construction of La Muralla, the city wall, began nearly 400 years ago.

©OMAR VEGA

© SUZANNE VAN ATTEN

Paseo de Princesa, a bayside promenade where festivals and events are frequently held

Paseo de Princesa. Named after La Princesa, a 19th-century prison that now houses the Puerto Rico Tourism Company, the promenade begins across from Plaza de Hostos at Calle Tizol near the cruise-ship piers in Old San Juan. Glorious royal palms, a view of the bay, the soaring city wall, the city gate, and an outlandish fountain comprising naked sea nymphs and goats are some of the sights along the way. The promenade continues along El Morro, ending dramatically at the point containing the oldest part of the fort. Paseo de Princesa is the site of frequent festivals and events, and you can usually find a variety of vendors here selling *piraguas* (snow cones), popcorn, and *dulces* (sweets).

Cuartel de Ballajá (Calle Norzagaray beside Plaza del Quinto Centenario near the entrance to El Morro, Old San Juan) is a massive structure that once housed 1,000 Spanish soldiers. Built in 1854, the former barracks are three levels high with interior balconies and a dizzying series of arches that overlook an enormous courtyard. It was the last major building constructed by the Spanish in the New World. Today it houses the Museo de Las Americas, featuring a fantastic folk art collection.

Cementerio de Santa María Magdalena de Pazzis is the city's historic cemetery, outside the city wall just east of El Morro and accessible from Calle Norzagaray in Old San Juan. In addition to a neoclassical chapel, there are many significant burial sites of some of the city's early colonists, as well as the tomb of Pedro Albizu Campos, the revered revolutionary who sought independence for the island of Puerto Rico. Avoid going alone or at night. Next door is **La Perla,** an impoverished community notorious for its drug trade; its illicit activities are known to spill over into the cemetery. If you don't want to venture in, you can get a great view of it from Plaza del Quinto Centenario on Calle Norzagaray.

Condado

Information about the small lagoon-based **Fuerte San Jerónimo** (behind Caribe Hilton in Puerta de Tierra) is difficult to come by, perhaps because it's the only fort in San Juan that isn't part of the San Juan National Historic

Site. Instead, it's overseen by the Institute of Puerto Rican Culture and managed by the Caribe Hilton, on whose property it now sits. Various sources date its origins to the 17th and 18th centuries. Unfortunately, it's rarely open to the public.

Greater San Juan

El Cañuelo (end of Carr. 870 on Isla de Cabras, Toa Alta, daily 8:30 A.M.–5:30 P.M., $2) is the ruins of a tiny fortress across the bay from El Morro. Originally constructed of wood in the 1500s, it was destroyed in an attack by the Dutch in 1625. The current stone structure was built in the 1670s. Its purpose was to work in concert with El Morro to create cannon cross-fire at the mouth of the bay. Unfortunately, the public is not allowed to enter the fort, but it provides a terrific view of El Morro. There's a small recreation area with picnic tables.

A few crumbling walls and foundations are all that's left of **Ruinas de Caparra** (Carr. 2, km 6.4, Guaynabo, 787/781-4795, Mon.–Fri. 9 A.M.–4 P.M.), the site of Juan Ponce de León's first settlement on the island, established in 1508. Attempts to develop the settlement didn't last long. The property is in a swamp that proved nearly uninhabitable, so settlers quickly relocated to Old San Juan. The small museum contains historical documents and Taíno artifacts pertaining to the site.

Rum plays a long, colorful role in the history and economic development of Puerto Rico. Established in 1862 by Don Facundo Bacardi Masó, Bacardi is the top-selling rum in the United States and is still owned and operated by its founder's descendants. For an interactive lesson on its production, **Casa Bacardi Visitor Center** (Carr. 165, km 6.2, Cataño, 787/788-8400, www.casabacardi .org, Mon.–Sat. 8:30 A.M.–5:30 P.M., last tour at 4:15 P.M.; Sun. 10 A.M.–5 P.M., last tour at 3:45 P.M., free) offers audiotaped tours of its largest distillery, bottling operation, and museum of historic artifacts. Admission includes two drinks and a trolley tour of the surrounding gardens. The factory is a 20-minute drive from San Juan. Alternatively, visitors can catch

the AquaExpreso ferry (6 A.M.–10 P.M., $0.50) at Pier 2 in Old San Juan to Cataño, where a *publico* van will provide transportation to the factory for $2–6, depending on the number of riders.

HISTORY MUSEUMS

Museo de Arte e Historia de San Juan (150 Calle Norzagaray, Old San Juan, 787/724-1875, Wed.–Fri. 9 A.M.–noon and 1–4 P.M., Sat.–Sun. 10 A.M.–4 P.M., free) is in the city's former marketplace, built in 1857. In 1979 it was converted into a city museum. It contains two exhibition spaces, one housing temporary exhibits illuminating various aspects of the city's history, the other a permanent exhibition that gives a comprehensive look at the city's history from its geographical roots to the 21st century. Superbly produced wall graphics and text include reproductions of old photographs, maps, prints, and paintings that tell the city's story. All the exhibits are in Spanish, but a photocopied handout in English encapsulates the exhibition highlights.

Two museums in one, **Casa de la Familia Puertorriqueña del Siglo XIX** and **Museo de la Farmacia** (319 Calle Fortaleza, Old San Juan, 787/977-2700 or 787/977-2701, Tues.–Sat. 8:30 A.M.–4:20 P.M., free) is a re-creation of a typical (albeit wealthy) family's residence from the late 1800s filled with antiques, both locally made and imported from Germany, Belgium, and Italy. Downstairs are vessels, cabinets, scales, and various other accoutrements from a 19th-century pharmacy in Cayey.

Museo de Nuestra Raíz Africana (Calle San Sebastían beside Plaza de San José, Old San Juan, 787/724-4294 or 787/724-4184, Tues.–Sat. 8:30 A.M.–4:20 P.M.) explores the African influence on Puerto Rican culture. Slavery and abolition figure prominently, including a display of handcuffs and collars and a simulated re-creation of what it was like to cross the ocean in a slave ship.

Museo del Indio (119 San José, Old San Juan, 787/721-2864, Tues.–Sat. 9:30 A.M.–3:30 P.M., free) is San Juan's newest museum. Devoted to the history of the island's Taíno Indian population, it contains many artifacts unearthed in excavations around the island including pottery, stone tools, and *cemies,* small carved stone talismans representative of various gods.

ART MUSEUMS AND GALLERIES
Santurce
◖ MUSEO DE ARTE DE PUERTO RICO

Without a doubt, the crowning jewel of San Juan's cultural institutions is Museo de Arte de Puerto Rico (299 Ave. José de Diego, Santurce, 787/977-6277, fax 787/977-4446, www.mapr .org, Tues. and Thurs.–Sat. 10 A.M.–5 P.M., Wed. 10 A.M.–8 P.M., Sun. 11 A.M.–6 P.M., $6 adults, $3 children 5–12, seniors, students with ID, and visitors with disabilities; valet parking). Visitors with even a passing interest in art will be bowled over by the volume and quality of work produced by the many gifted artists who hail from this small island.

The modern, new 130,000-square-foot, neoclassical structure opened in 2000 and is devoted to Puerto Rican art from the 17th century to the present. And joy! The wall text is in Spanish and English. Exhibition highlights include works by the celebrated Francisco Manuel Oller, a European-trained 17th-century realist-impressionist, and a striking selection of *cartels,* a mid-century poster-art form distinguished by bold graphics and socially conscious themes.

Contemporary art is on the second floor, and it is not to be missed. One room is devoted to Rafael Trelles's 1957 installation *Visits to the Wake,* inspired by Oller's famous 19th-century painting of a family attending a child's wake, called *El Veloria.* The piece combines video, sculpture, found objects, and life-size cutouts of the painting's characters to astounding effect. Another remarkable work is Pepón Osorio's installation titled *No Crying Allowed in the Barbershop.* The simulated barbershop explores issues of male vanity, rites of passage, and early lessons in masculinity.

There are also temporary exhibition spaces for rotating shows, a children's gallery, a five-acre modern sculpture garden, and the Raul

Julia Theater, featuring an intriguing curtain made of mundillo, a traditional handmade lace. A museum shop is also on-site, as is Pikayo, a pricey fine-dining restaurant.

OTHER ART MUSEUMS AND GALLERIES

Before Museo de Arte de Puerto Rico opened, **Museo de Arte Contemporáneo de Puerto Rico** (Escuela Rafael M. de Labra, corner of Roberto H. Todd and Ponce de León, Santurce, 787/977-4030, 787/977-4031, or 787/977-4032, www.museocontemporaneo pr.org, Tues.–Sat. 10 A.M.–4 P.M., Sun. noon–4 P.M., free) was the place to go for modern art. Unfortunately, it's a bit of a disappointment in comparison. But it's worth a visit just to see the building, an atypical red-brick Georgian structure completed in 1918. Two small exhibition spaces feature rotating exhibits from the permanent collection. Wall text is in Spanish only.

Espacio 1414 (1414 Ave. Fernández Juncos, 787/725-3899, www.espacio1414.com, Sat. 2 P.M.–6 P.M.) is a contemporary art space established in a former warehouse. In addition to its permanent collection of contemporary Latin American art, it features three levels of temporary exhibition space.

Old San Juan
MUSEO DE LAS AMERICAS

The other side of the art pendulum from Museo de Arte de Puerto Rico is Museo de Las Americas (Cuartel de Ballajá, second floor, on Calle Norzagaray beside Plaza del Quinto Centenario, Old San Juan, 787/724-5052, fax 787/722-2848, musame@prtc.net, www .prtc.net/~musame, Tues.–Fri. 10 A.M.–4 P.M., Sat.–Sun. 11 A.M.–5 P.M., free). Inside an enormous structure that once housed 1,000 Spanish soldiers, the museum contains a fantastic collection of Latin American folk art, including masks, musical instruments, clothing, pottery, baskets, and tools. Highlights include altars representing Santeria, voodoo, and Mexico's Day of the Dead celebration. Don't miss the collection of vintage Santos, Puerto Rican wood carvings of saints.

Wall text is in Spanish and English except in the second smaller exhibit dedicated to Puerto Rico's African heritage. The **Tienda de Artesanías** on the first floor (Tues.–Fri. 10 A.M.–4 P.M., Sat.–Sun. 11 A.M.–5 P.M., 787/722-6057) has a small but quality selection of locally made crafts for sale.

OTHER ART MUSEUMS AND GALLERIES

La Casa de Libro (255 Calle Cristo, Old San Juan, 787/723-0354, lcdl@prw.net, www.lacasa dellibro.org, Tues.–Sat. 11:30 A.M.–4:30 P.M., free) is a little gem of a museum in a former residence. It has an impressive collection of historic books displayed in exhibits that rotate about every three months. In 2005 it featured an exhibit honoring the 400-year anniversary of Cervantes's *Don Quixote* that included a first edition from 1605.

Museo Pablo Casals (101 Calle San Sebastían, Old San Juan, 787/723-9185, Tues.–Sat. 9:30 A.M.–5:30 P.M., $1) commemorates the career and accomplishments of Pablo Casals, the renowned cellist who performed for Queen Victoria and President Theodore Roosevelt, among other world movers and shakers. Born in Catalonia, Casals moved to Puerto Rico in 1956. A year later, the island established the annual Casals Festival of classical music, which continues today. Inside an 18th-century building, the museum contains Casals's music manuscripts, cello, and piano. You can hear recordings of Casals performing in the music room upstairs.

One of the oldest theaters in the Western Hemisphere is **Teatro Tapia** (Calle Fortaleza at Plaza de Colón, Old San Juan, 787/721-0180 or 787/721-0169), a lovely Romantic-style building constructed in 1824 and renovated in 1987. Named after Puerto Rican playwright Alejandro Tapia y Rivera, the 642-seat theater still hosts a variety of performance art events.

Several interesting galleries are in Old San Juan. Among the best is **Galeria Botello** (208 Calle Cristo, Old San Juan, 787/723-9987 or 787/723-2879, fax 787/724-6776, botellosj@msn.com, www.botello.com, Mon.–Sat. 10 A.M.–6 P.M.). Although he was born in Spain, renowned artist Angel Botello spent most of his life in the Caribbean, eventually settling in Puerto Rico, where he opened this gallery. Although he died in 1986, the artist lives on through his paintings and sculptures on view at the gallery, which also exhibits solo shows by contemporary artists. **Galeria Exodo** (200-B Calle Cristo, Old San Juan, 787/725-4252 or 787/671-4159, galeriaexodo@gmail.com, www .galeriaexodo.com, Mon.–Fri. 11 A.M.–7 P.M., Sat. 10 A.M.–6 P.M., Sun. 11 A.M.–5 P.M.)— formerly Fósil Arte—has a wide diversity of mostly high-quality works by contemporary artists, both Puerto Rican and international. **The Butterfly People** (257 Calle de la Cruz, Old San Juan, 787/723-2432 or 787/723-2201, info@butterflypeople.com, www.butterfly people.com, 10 A.M.–6 P.M. daily) is a unique gallery that sells fantastic colorful pieces composed of real butterflies mounted in Lucite.

RELIGIOUS SITES

◖ Catedral de San Juan Bautista

Catedral de San Juan Bautista (151–153 Calle del Cristo, Old San Juan, 787/722-0861, www.catedralsanjuan.com, Mon.–Thurs. 9 A.M.–noon and 1:30–4 P.M., Fri. 9 A.M.– noon; Mass Sat. 9 A.M., 11 A.M., and 7 P.M., Sun.–Fri. 12:15 P.M.) holds the distinction of being the second-oldest church in the western hemisphere, the first being Catedral Basilica Menor de Santa in the Dominican Republic. The church was first built of wood and straw in 1521 but was destroyed by hurricanes and rebuilt multiple times. In 1917 the cathedral underwent major restoration and expansion. The large sanctuary features a marble altar and rows of arches with several side chapels appointed with elaborate statuary primarily depicting Mary and Jesus. In stark contrast is a chapel featuring an enormous contemporary oil painting of a man in a business suit. It was erected in honor of Carlos "Charlie" Rodríguez, a Puerto Rican layman who was beatified in 2001 by Pope John Paul II. Catedral de San Juan Bautista is the final resting place of Juan de Ponce de León, whose remains are encased in a marble tomb, and a relic of San Pio, a Roman martyr.

© OMAR VEGA

Capilla del Cristo is a tiny chapel at the end of Calle de la Cristo overlooking San Juan Bay.

Capilla del Cristo

Built in 1753, the tiny picturesque Capilla del Cristo (south end of Calle de la Cristo, Old San Juan, 787/722-0861) is one of the most photographed sights in San Juan. Legend has it that horse races were held on Calle del Cristo, and one ill-fated rider was speeding down the hill so fast he couldn't stop in time and tumbled over the city wall to his death, and the chapel was built to prevent a similar occurrence. An alternative end to the legend is that the rider survived and the church was built to show thanks to God. Either way, the result was the construction of a beloved landmark.

Unfortunately, Capilla del Cristo is rarely open, but it's possible to peer through the windows and see the ornate gilded altarpiece. Beside it is **Parque de Palomas,** a gated park overlooking San Juan Harbor that is home to more pigeons than you might think imaginable. Bird seed is available for purchase if you want to get up close and personal with your fine feathered friends.

Iglesia San José

Although Catedral de San Juan Bautista gets all the glory, Iglesia San José (Calle San Sebastían at Plaza de San José, Old San Juan, 787/725-7501) is one of the oldest structures in Old San Juan. Built in the 1530s, it was originally a chapel for the Dominican monastery, but it was taken over in 1865 by the Jesuits. The main chapel is an excellent example of 16th-century Spanish Gothic architecture. Originally Iglesia San José was Juan Ponce de León's final resting place, but his body was later moved to Catedral de San Juan Bautista. Ponce de León himself is said to have donated the wooden 16th-century crucifix. Unfortunately, the church has been closed for many years while it undergoes a seemingly endless renovation project.

FAMILY ATTRACTIONS

El Jardín Botánico (Hwy. 1 at Carr. 847 in Río Piedras, 787/250-0000, ext. 6578, or 787/767-1701, daily 6 A.M.–6 P.M., free, guides available by special arrangement 10 A.M.–1 P.M.) is a 289-acre urban garden filled with tropical and subtropical vegetation, including orchids, heliconias, bromeliads, palms, and bamboo. There's also a native Taíno garden display of native plants. It is maintained by the University of Puerto Rico.

For hands-on educational activities geared toward children, head to **Museo del Niño** (150 Calle Cristo near El Convento Hotel, Old San Juan, 787/722-3791, info@museodelninopr.org, www.museodelninopr.org, Tues.–Thurs. 9 A.M.–3:30 P.M., Fri. 9 A.M.–5 P.M., Sat.–Sun. 12:30–5 P.M., $5 adults, $7 children). This three-story museum contains exhibits in geography, nutrition, weather, astronomy, biology, and more.

An even more elaborate interactive educational opportunity can be found at **Parque de las Ciencias Luis A. Ferré** (Carr. 167, off Hwy. 22 in Bayamón, 787/740-6878, 787/740-6868, 787/740-6869, or 787/740-6871, Wed.–Fri. 9 A.M.–4 P.M., Sat.–Sun. and holidays 10 A.M.–6 P.M., ticket booth closes two hours before park closing, $5 adults, $3 children, $2.50 seniors 65 and older and those with disabilities; parking $1; planetarium $3 adults, $2 children). Basically an amusement park devoted to science, it encompasses 37 acres and features an aerospace museum with NASA rockets, a natural-science museum, an art museum, a small zoo, a planetarium, an archaeology museum, a transportation museum, a lake with paddleboats, and food vendors selling hot dogs and pizza.

PLAZAS AND PARKS

Colonial Spanish towns are traditionally anchored by a plaza that serves as an important gathering place for the community, and Old San Juan is lucky enough to have several. There's no better way to spend the morning than strolling the perimeter of a plaza or spending time on a bench sipping coffee, fending off pigeons, and watching the parade of people pass by. The plazas are also popular sites for arts festivals and evening concerts.

Metropolitan San Juan also has several modern parks with all the jogging trails and children's playgrounds modern man (or woman) could want.

Artisans rolling handmade cigars can be found in the plazas of Old San Juan.

Old San Juan

Not surprisingly, the largest concentration of historic plazas and parks is in Old San Juan. **Plaza de Armas** (Calle San Francisco, at Calle de la Cruz and Calle San José) is the main square in Old San Juan and a great place to people-watch. Once the site of military drills, it contains a large gazebo and a fountain surrounded by four 100-year-old statues that represent the four seasons. A couple of vendors sell coffee and snacks, and there's a bank of pay phones popular with cruise-ship visitors eager to check in with those back home. Across the street on Calle de la Cruz is a small grocery store. Across Calle Cordero is an ATM, and a taxi stand is just around the corner on Calle San José at Calle Fortaleza.

Plaza de Colón (between Calle Fortaleza, Calle San Francisco, and Calle O'Donnell) is a large square at the entrance to Old San Juan by San Cristóbal fortress. In the center is a huge pedestal topped with a statue of Christopher Columbus, whom the plaza is named after.

There's a small newsstand on one corner, and several restaurants and shops surround it on two sides. Unfortunately, there's little shade, so it's not that pleasant for lingering when the sun is high.

Old San Juan's newest square is **Plaza del Quinto Centenario** (between Calle Norzagaray and Calle Beneficencia near the entrance to El Morro, Old San Juan). Built to commemorate the 500th anniversary of Christopher Columbus's "discovery" of the New World, the plaza features a striking 40-foot totem made from black granite and ceramic pieces created by local artist Jaime Suárez. The plaza provides a great view of the historic cemetery, El Morro, and all the kite flyers who gather on the fort's long green lawn.

One of Puerto Rico's most beautiful pieces of public art is in **Plazuela de la Rogativa,** a tiny sliver of a park tucked between the city wall and Calle Clara Lair just west of El Convento in Old San Juan. At its center is a spectacular bronze sculpture called *La Rogativa,* designed by New Zealand artist Lindsay Daen in the 1950s. The piece depicts a procession of three women and a priest bearing crosses and torches. It commemorates one of San Juan's most beloved historic tales. In 1797 a British fleet led by Sir Ralph Abercrombie entered San Juan Bay and prepared to launch an attack in hopes of capturing the city. Because the city's men were away protecting the city's inland fronts, the only people remaining behind were women and clergy. In hopes of staving off an attack, the governor ordered a *rogativa,* a divine entreaty to ask the saints for help. As the story goes, the town's brave women formed a procession, carrying torches and ringing bells throughout the streets, which duped the British into thinking reinforcements had arrived, prompting them to sail away, leaving the city safe once again.

Plaza de José (Calle San Sebastían and Calle Cristo, Old San Juan) is in front of the Iglesia de San José and features a statue of its most celebrated parishioner, Juan Ponce de León. After successfully thwarting another attack by the British in 1797, citizens of San Juan melted the enemy's cannons to make the statue. This is a popular gathering place for young locals, especially at night when the string of nearby bars gets crowded.

Plaza de Hostos (between Calle San Justo and Calle Tizol, Old San Juan) is a bustling shady spot near the cruise-ship piers. On weekends it turns into a craft fair, and there are often food vendors selling fritters and snow cones. Just across the street, at **Plaza Dársenas,** concerts are often held on the weekends on a covered stage overlooking the harbor.

Beside Capilla de Cristo on the south end of Calle de la Cristo in Old San Juan is **Parque de Palomas,** a small gated park packed with a zillion pigeons. A vendor sells small bags of feed for those who take pleasure in being swarmed with the feathered urban dwellers. Kids love it!

Condado

Aside from its long stretch of beach, Condado is mostly concrete and asphalt, but there are several very nice, compact parks there. **Ventanas al Mar, Plaza Ancla,** and **Parque del Indio** are all on the ocean side of Avenida Ashford, and although they're primarily concrete, they feature excellent pieces of contemporary public art, benches for resting, and access to the water. Plaza Ancla has the added bonus of a terrific open-air restaurant, Barlovento, which has a full bar and serves Mediterranean cuisine. Another waterside park between Condado and Miramar is **Parque Laguna del Condado** (by Dos Hermanos bridge). Having recently undergone a $500,000 renovation, the park features hiking, biking, and jogging trails that run along Condado Lagoon and has kayak rentals available.

Condado's best park, though, is **Parque Luchetti** (between Calle Magdalena and Calle Luchetti at Calle Cervantes), a lovely oasis of quiet and lush green flora just two blocks away from the hubbub of Avenida Ashford. Shaded benches, flowering shrubs, palm trees, and public art make this the perfect spot to relax or picnic. One of the highlights is a whimsical bronze sculpture called *Juan Bobo and the Basket.* Created in 1991 by New Zealand artist Lindsay Daen, who made the more famous *La Rogativa* statue in Old San Juan, it's inspired by a local fable.

Puerta de Tierra

Puerta de Tierra is a spot of land between Condado and Old San Juan that is home to **Parque Luis Muñoz Rivera** (between Ave. Ponce de León and Ave. Muñoz Rivera), another lovely green space that provides a welcome reprieve from the city's urban atmosphere. Shady gardens, fountains, walking trails, a children's play area, and the Peace Pavilion can be found in this 27-acre park.

Ocean Park

Ocean Park's **Parque Barbosa** (end of Calle McLeary) isn't the prettiest or best-maintained park in San Juan, but it does have hiking, jogging, and bike paths. Its proximity to a large public-housing project may deter some visitors, but it's the perfect place to park when visiting Ocean Park beach, which is right across the street.

Hato Rey

Parque Luis Muñoz Marín (off Hwy. 18 between Ave. Jesús Piñero and Ave. F. D. Roosevelt, Wed.–Sun. and holidays) in Hato Rey is a modern 140-acre park with walking and bike trails, a children's play area, golf practice grounds, an amphitheater, pavilions, and more.

Sports and Recreation

When it comes to water sports, San Juan pales in comparison to the rest of Puerto Rico, but there are many tour operators in the area that will provide transportation to nearby sweet spots for snorkeling, diving, fishing, and more.

DIVING AND SNORKELING

Ocean Sports (77 Ave. Isla Verde, 787/268-2329, www.osdivers.com, Mon.–Sat. 10 A.M.–7 P.M.) rents and sells snorkel and scuba equipment from its two stores and operates scuba and snorkel tours from Fajardo. Road transportation to and from San Juan is available. **Caribbean School of Aquatics** (1 Calle Taft, 787/728-6606 or 787/383-5700, greg@saildiveparty.com, www.saildiveparty.com) offers full- and half-day sail, scuba, snorkel, and fishing trips from San Juan and Fajardo on a luxury catamaran with Captain Greg Korwek. Snorkel trips start at $79 per person; scuba trips start at $139 per person. **Scuba Dogs** (D-13 Buen Samaritano Gardenville, Guaynabo, 787/783-6377, www.scubadogs.net) provides scuba and snorkeling trips all around the island for everyone from first-timers to

those seeking PADI dive training. It also sells and rents equipment. **Caribe Aquatic Adventures** (Hotel Normandie, 499 W. Ave. Muñoz Rivera, 787/281-8858 or 787/724-1882, www.diveguide.com/p2046.htm) offers snorkel and reef dives four times daily, as well as light-tackle and deep-sea fishing trips.

SURFING

Costazul (264 Calle San Francisco, Old San Juan, 787/722-0991 or 787/724-8085, fax 787/725-1097, sferco@caribe.net, Mon.–Sat. 9 A.M.–7 P.M.) sells surfboards and related equipment. But if you need instruction, **Caribbean Surf School** (787/637-8363, www.caribbeansurfpr.com) offers daily and weekly lessons with avid surfers and certified lifeguards at various locations. The school has a 3:1 student-to-instructor ratio, as well as individual instruction.

Velauno (2430 Calle Loíza, San Juan, 787/982-0543 or 866/PR-VELA-1— 866/778-3521, www.velauno.com) is the go-to place for all things surfing, including kite-surfing and windsurfing. They sell and rent equipment and offer lessons for adults

© OMAR VEGA

windsurfing in Condado

and children, including weeklong summer camps for windsurfers.

BOATING

There are three marinas in San Juan, the largest being **San Juan Bay Marina** (787/721-8062), with a capacity of 191 boats, including 125 wet slips, 60 dry-stack spaces, and six spaces for yachts more than 100 feet long. There's also a restaurant on-site. **Club Náutico de San Juan** (787/722-0177) has 117 wet slips and **Congrejas Yacht Club** in Piñones (787/791-1015) has 180 wet slips, a boat ramp, and a restaurant. All three have fuel and water.

FISHING

Mike Benitez Marina Services (Club Náutico de San Juan, 787/723-2292 or 787/724-6265, fax 787/725-4344, Fishpr2001@yahoo.com, www.mikebenitezfishingpr.com) offers deep-sea fishing trips daily. Half-day trips last 8 A.M.–noon and 1–5 P.M. Full-day excursions depart at 8 A.M. and return at 4 P.M. Reservations are required, and there's a six-passenger maximum.

Caribbean Outfitters (Congrejas Yacht Club, 787/396-8346, www.fishinginpuertorico.com/captbig.htm) offers fishing and fly-fishing charters throughout Puerto Rico, Vieques, Culebra, the Dominican Republic, and St. Thomas with Captain Omar.

ADVENTURE SPORTS

The go-to outfitters for rappelling in the rain forest, cave tubing, zipline rides, and hiking is **EcoQuest** (New San Juan Building 6471, Suite 5A, Isla Verde, 787/616-7543 or 787/529-2496, info@ecoquest.com, www.ecoquestpr.com).

TENNIS

There is no shortage of tennis courts in San Juan. Many of the large hotels have courts. In addition, there are several public courts, including: **Caribbean Mountain Villas Tennis Court** (Carr. 857, km 857, Canovanillas Sector, Carolina, 787/769-0860); **Central Park** (Calle Cerra off Carr. 2, Santurce, 787/722-1646); **Isla Verde Tennis Club** (Villamar, Isla Verde, 787/727-6490).

SPAS

Eden Spa (331 Recinto Sur, bldg. Acosta, Old San Juan, 787/721-6400, www.secretsofeden spa.net, Mon.–Sat. 10 A.M.–7 P.M., VIP services 7–9 P.M.) offers pure luxury pampering, including caviar facials, four-hands massage, honey-butter body wrap, chakra-balancing treatments, Reiki—you name it, Eden Spa has got it.

Zen Spa (1054 Ave. Ashford, Condado, 787/722-8433, www.zen-spa.com, Mon.–Fri. 7 A.M.–9 P.M., Sat. 8 A.M.–6 P.M., Sun. 9 A.M.–6 P.M.) offers massage, body wraps, facials, manicures, and hair care. Day-spa packages run $125–400. There's also a health club on the premises.

Entertainment and Events

FESTIVALS

San Juan loves a festival. It seems as though there's one going on every weekend. Some have traditional origins, and others are products of the local tourism department, but they all promise insight into the island's culture and are loads of fun.

Noches de Galerias (787/723-7080) is held the first Tuesday of the month February–May and September–December. Roughly 20 museums and galleries throughout Old San Juan open 6–9 P.M. for this festive gallery crawl. Though its intentions may be high-minded, as the night progresses the event becomes more of a raucous pub crawl as young adults and teenagers fill the streets in revelry. Arts and crafts booths also line Plaza de San José.

Held in June, **Noche de San Juan Bautista** is the celebration of the island's patron saint. Festivities last several days and include religious processions, concerts, and dance performances. But the highlight of the event is on June 24, when celebrants from all over the island flock to the beach for the day for picnics and recreation. Then at midnight, everyone walks backward into the ocean three times to ward off evil spirits.

Founded in honor of the renowned cellist and composer Pablo Casals, the **Festival Casals** (787/725-7334) is held in June and July and features a slate of classical music concerts at the Fine Arts Center (Ave. de Diego at Ave. Ponce de León). Concerts are also held in Ponce and Mayagüez.

Street festivals don't get any more lively

than **Festival de la Calle de San Sebastián** (787/724-0910), held in January on Calle San Sebastían in Old San Juan. For three days the street is filled with parades, folkloric dances, music, food, and crafts.

Each year the **Heineken Jazz Festival** (Anfiteatro Tito Puente in Hato Rey, 866/994-0001) selects a single jazz master to celebrate with three nights of concerts, 8 P.M.–midnight.

The Puerto Rico Tourism Company presents an annual three-day arts festival in early June called **Feria de Artesanías** (787/723-0692, www.gotopuertorico.com). More than 200 artisans fill the walkways along Paseo La Princesa and Plaza Dársena, and the days are filled with music and dance performances as well as a folk-singer competition.

Less an actual festival and more a cultural series, **La Casita Festival** takes place every Saturday 5:30–7:30 P.M. year-round in Plaza de la Dársena by Pier 1 in Old San Juan. Musicians and dance groups perform, and artisans sell their wares.

Similarly, **LeLoLai Festival** (787/723-3135, 787/791-1014, or 800/223-6530) presents traditional concerts and dance performances year-round at various sites throughout the island, including InterContinental Hotel San Juan in Isla Verde and Castillo de San Cristóbal in Old San Juan.

NIGHTLIFE

If club- and bar-hopping is your thing, you've come to the right place. San Juan definitely knows how to party. The most popular nightclubs and bars tend to be in Old San Juan, Condado, Santurce, and Isla Verde. Electronic music is prevalent, as is reggaetón, Puerto Rico's homegrown brand of hip-hop, combined with Jamaican dancehall and Caribbean musical styles. The legal drinking age is 18, and there's no official bar-closing time, so many establishments stay open until 6 A.M. Things don't really get started until after midnight, so take a disco nap and put on your dancing shoes. It's sure to be a long fun-filled night.

Old San Juan
◖ NUYORICAN CAFÉ
By far the best nightclub for live contemporary Latin music—from rock and jazz to salsa and merengue—is Nuyorican Café (312 Calle San Francisco, 787/977-1276, Tues.–Wed. 7 P.M.–3 A.M., Thurs.–Sun. 7 P.M.–5 A.M., free every night except $5 Fri., full bar). Don't bother looking for a sign; there isn't one. Just look for a gaggle of club-goers clustered around a side door down Capilla alley, which connects Calle San Francisco and Calle Fortaleza. Primarily a locals' place, although tourists are welcome, this casual music-lovers' club packs in a young bohemian crowd, especially on weekends when the tiny dance floor gets jammed. The kitchen serves a limited menu of Puerto Rican cuisine until midnight. The music usually starts around 11 P.M. There's no direct link between this café and New York City's Nuyorican Poets Café, which was and still is the epicenter of the Nuyorican movement, although the name is a nod to the club in New York City.

OTHER BARS AND CLUBS
San Juan's hippest nightclub scene revolves around electronic music and reggaetón, and there are any number of clubs devoted to the forms. Old San Juan's veteran nightclub is **Club Lazer** (251 Calle de la Cruz, 787/725-7581, www.clublazer.com, Wed.–Sun. 10 P.M.–3 or 4 A.M.). The three-level 1980s-era disco complete with a light show is popular with both gays and straights. The hottest DJs spin here, and Sunday is reggaetón night.

The hottest new dance club for the young techno crowd is **Milk** (314 Calle Fortaleza, 787/721-3548, www.myspace.com/clubmilkpr, Thurs.–Sat. 10 P.M.–5 A.M.). The narrow, two-level spot sports a chic minimalist look, and patrons are expected to dress to impress—no baggy jeans, baseball caps, flip-flops, sneakers, or tank tops allowed. DJs spin all night long, and there's great people-watching from the balcony. Reservations required for table service.

Raven Room (305 Recinto Sur, 787/667-9651, www.ravenroompr.com, Wed.–Sat. 10 P.M.–3 or 4 A.M., $7), formerly Oleo Lounge, is a popular new club for the 21 and up set featuring minimalist decor and DJs spinning everything from the latest dance tunes to hits from the '70s and '80s.

The Noise (203 Calle Tanca, 787/724-3739) is a white-hot club in a former house in Old San Juan, where reggaetón keeps the beat going until the wee hours. Popular with the 18–21 crowd.

Blend (309 Calle Fortaleza, 787/977-7777, Tues.–Sat. 5 P.M.–3:30 A.M.) is a chic restaurant and lounge centered around an indoor patio and dramatic wall fountain. Local and touring DJs spin all forms of techno.

Club Le Cirque (357 Calle San Francisco, 787/725-3246, Wed.–Sat. 6 P.M.–4 A.M.) is a gay bar and lounge serving lunch and dinner. Smoking is allowed on the patio.

Another popular late-night bar for the casual bohemian crowd is **Galeria Candela** (110 Calle San Sebastian, 787/594-5698 or 787/977-4305). The space is a hipster art gallery by day, but at night DJs spin into the wee hours.

If you need a place to rest your feet and just chill with a cool beverage, there is a wide variety of bars, both casual and upscale, where you can actually have a conversation, at least in the early part of the evening. The later it gets, though, the more crowded and louder it gets.

Although primarily an Indo-Latino fusion restaurant, **Tantra** (356 Calle Fortaleza, 787/977-8141, fax 787/977-4289, www.tantra pr.com, Sun.–Thurs. noon–11 P.M., Fri.–Sat.

noon–midnight) turns into a late-night party spot for the hip and trendy after-dinner crowd who flock here for the sophisticated ambiance, the creative martinis, and a toke or two on one of the many hookahs that line the bar. The kitchen serves a limited late-night menu.

For something completely different, frozen tropical drinks and old kitschy decor create the perfect place for a shopping break at **María's** (204 Calle de la Cristo, no telephone, daily 10:30 A.M.–3 A.M.). The tiny, pleasantly seedy bar primarily serves a variety of frozen drinks—piña colada, papaya frost, coconut blossom, and so on (with or without rum). Avoid the pedestrian tacos and nachos ($3.75–7) and check out the cheesy celebrity photos behind the bar. If the dark, narrow bar is full, there are a couple of tables in the back.

Looking for all the world like an old jail cell, **El Batey** (101 Calle Cristo, 787/725-1787, daily noon–4 A.M., cash only) is a barren dive bar covered top to bottom with drunken-scrawled graffiti and illuminated by bare bulbs suspended from the ceiling. There's one pool table and an interesting jukebox with lots of jazz mixed in with classic discs by the likes of Tom Waits, Jimi Hendrix, and Sly Stone. If you order a martini, they'll laugh at you. This is a beer and shots kind of place.

The barred windows and garish orange exterior don't offer much of a welcome at **Krugger** (52 Calle San José, 787/723-2474, Thurs.–Sat.), but the word is that this loud dive bar is the place to go for karaoke.

Isla Verde

One of San Juan's most glamorous bars is **❰ Wet,** atop the Water Club hotel (2 Calle Tartak, 787/728-3666 or 888/265-6699, fax 787/728-3610, www.waterclubsanjuan.com). This posh rooftop bar looks like the set for *The Real World,* and the clientele are just as young and trendy as that show's cast members. Huge white leather sofas and beds arranged around tiny tables under a white awning set the tone for its chill vibe. The minimal lighting is limited to elaborate Indonesian lanterns and candles, which complement the panoramic view of

the city lights. Sushi and supersweet martinis, with porn-star names such as Mango Do Me and Mojito Lips, are typical fare. If you need further proof that this is the place to see and be seen, Donatella Versace was reportedly spotted in the ladies' room.

On the first floor of The Water Club is **Liquid,** a more intimate bar that shares space with the hotel's restaurant, Tangerine. The attraction here is the interesting wall behind the bar—it's made from corrugated tin over which water pours all night long.

Another popular hotel hotspot is **Brava** (Wyndham El San Juan Hotel, 6063 Ave. Isla Verde, 787/791-2761 or 787/791-2781, www.bravapr.com). Formerly Club Babylon, this popular dance club still packs in the upscale trendy set, who dance to an eclectic mix of dance-club tunes, salsa, and '80s rock. Reservations required for table service.

For something more casual, **Drums** (Isla Verde Mall, 787/253-1443, www.drums puertorico.com, Mon.–Tues. 11 A.M.–11 P.M., Wed. 11 A.M.–1 A.M., Thurs. 11 A.M.–2 A.M., Fri.–Sat. 11 A.M.–4 A.M., Sun. 11:30 A.M.–2:30 A.M.) is a huge, crowded spot that packs 'em in for live rock music, DJs, and karaoke. It serves an extensive menu of pub grub, as well entrées including steak, fish, and ribs.

Condado

The large open-air pavilion bar **La Terraza Condado** (intersection of Ave. Ashford and Calle McLeary, 787/723-2770, Sun.–Thurs. 5 P.M.–midnight, Fri.–Sat. 5 P.M.–2 A.M.) is popular with a young crowd that flocks here on the weekends for the cheap drinks, and it's an ideal perch for people-watching. There's a full bar, and it serves Puerto Rican cuisine ($9–18).

There are two types of strip clubs in Puerto Rico—those that don't serve alcohol and feature nude dancers, and those that serve alcohol and feature dancers who keep their G-strings on. **Divas** (1104 Ave. Ashford, 787/721-8270, www.myspace.com/divasinternational, $10) is the latter. Fairly upscale and well controlled by several large no-nonsense men in suits, it's a safe, saucy environment that attracts both men and women. It features a full bar and a private VIP room upstairs.

Santurce

Santurce's club scene primarily serves the gay community, but beware that it can be a rough part of town, especially at night. Panhandlers and petty thieves are known to prowl the area, so take precautions.

Santurce is home to several gay clubs. **Krash** (1257 Ave. Ponce de León, 787/722-1131, www.krashpr.com, Wed.–Sat. 10 P.M.–3 A.M., $6 after midnight), formerly Eros, is a major two-level party scene. Wednesday is urban pop night with three DJs spinning R&B, hip-hop, and reggaetón. Thursday and Friday nights feature DJs spinning house, tribal, and retro.

For a casual low-key gay bar, check out **Junior's Bar** (613 Calle Condado, 787/723-9477, daily, two-drink minimum). This is the place to have a beer, play some tunes on the jukebox, and check out the occasional drag queen or male stripper show.

Yet another popular gay bar and lounge in Santurce is **Starz** (365 Ave. de Diego, 787/721-8645).

The local lesbian crowd gathers in the laid-back ambiance of **Cups** (1708 Calle San Mateo, 787/268-3570, Wed.–Fri. 7 P.M.–3 A.M., Sat. 8 P.M.–3 A.M.). DJs spin dance music on Wednesday nights, karaoke is Thursday nights, and live music is Friday nights. There are pool tables too.

Hato Rey

For a little taste of España, check out the Saturday night flamenco show at ◖ **Divino Bocadito** (574 Ave. Ponce de Leon, Hato Rey, 787/765-8282, www.divinobocadito .com, Wed.–Thurs. 11 A.M.–midnight, Fri. 11 A.M.–2 A.M., Sat. 7 P.M.–2 A.M., Sun. 7 P.M.–midnight). Formerly located in Old San Juan, this lively Spanish bar and restaurant serves tapas and paella, but the real reason to come is to dance. Flamenco shows are Saturdays at 9 P.M., Andalusian dance performances are Thursdays and Fridays at 8 P.M., and dance classes are Wednesdays 7:30–8:30 P.M.

PARTY DISTRICTS

There's no doubt about it: Puerto Ricans love a good party, and it seems as if there's always one going on somewhere. San Juan has a couple of unofficial party districts where the concentration of bars and restaurants creates a street-party atmosphere that attracts young locals and tourists alike to barhop and people-watch. Although generally safe and contained, these areas can experience a certain level of rowdiness and petty crime, particularly when heavy drinking is involved. Visitors are encouraged to have a good time, but they should take care to keep their wits about them.

One popular party spot just a short taxi ride from Condado is **Plaza del Mercado** (Calle Roberts in Santurce), a small grid of narrow streets that surround Santurce's historic marketplace. The area contains a high concentration of tiny bars and restaurants serving cheap drinks and local cuisine. The streets get especially crowded Thursday, Friday, and Saturday nights with locals celebrating the weekend. If the walk-up bars and street scene get to be

Plaza del Mercado in Santurce

too much, duck into **Buyé Bistro Criolla** (202 Calle Canals, by Plaza del Mercado, Santurce, 787/725-4826, Mon.–Wed. 1–3 P.M., Thurs.–Fri. 1–3 P.M. and 5 P.M.–1 A.M., Sat. 5 P.M.–1 A.M.), especially on a Friday night. DJs spin here until the wee hours of the morning at this casual bar and restaurant. Check the chalkboard for daily specials ($7.95–16.95).

Another popular party district is **Boca de Cangrejas** (end of Ave. Isla Verde, just past the airport), a sandy patch of beachfront bars, restaurants, clubs, and food kiosks. Since this is also a popular weekend beach spot, the party tends to start early here, but the fun still lasts late into the night. The best way to get to Boca de Cangrejas is to drive or take a taxi, although you'll have to call one to pick you up when you're ready to leave. If you drive, be sure not to leave anything of value visible in the car; break-ins are not uncommon.

Although most establishments are open-air concrete structures, there are a few more-upscale places, such as **Soleil Beach Club** (Carr. 187, km 4.6, 787/253-1033, www.soleilbeach club.com, Sun.–Thurs. 11 A.M.–11 P.M., Fri.–Sat. 11 A.M.–2 A.M.), near Boca de Cangrejas in Piñones. The beachside establishment with the palm-frond entrance serves Puerto Rican cuisine and offers live Latin music.

In Old San Juan, party central is along **Calle San Sebastián.** Bars, clubs, and pool halls of every stripe line the street, making it a great place to barhop door-to-door. Standard stops include **Nono's** (109 Calle San Sebastián, 787/725-7819, daily noon–2 A.M.) and **Cafe San Sebastián** (153 Calle San Sebastián, 787/725-3998, Wed.–Sun. 8 P.M.–3 A.M.).

CASINOS

Puerto Rico's greatest concentration of casinos can be found in San Juan. It has a total of 10 gambling palaces, all in hotels. Although jacket and tie are not required, attire tends to be dressy. All the casinos have banks of slot machines, blackjack tables, and roulette wheels. Most have craps tables, Caribbean stud poker, and three-card poker. Some have mini-baccarat, let it ride, progressive blackjack, and Texas hold 'em.

The largest casino is at the **Ritz-Carlton San Juan Hotel** (Isla Verde, 787/253-1700, 10 A.M.–6 A.M.). Within its 17,000 square feet are 335 slots, 11 blackjack tables, four mini-baccarat games, and Texas hold 'em. **Wyndham El San Juan Hotel** (787/791-1000, 10 P.M.–4 A.M.) has the largest number of blackjack tables—14—and the added bonus of proximity to one of the most glamorous old-school hotel lobbies on the island, filled with gorgeous ornate woodwork and a massive antique chandelier. The only 24-hour casino in Isla Verde is **Courtyard by Marriott** (787/791-0404). Other casinos in the area include **InterContinental San Juan** (787/791-6100, 10 A.M.–4 A.M.) and **Embassy Suites Hotel** (787/791-0505, 10 A.M.–4 A.M.).

For a concentration of casino action, Condado is the place to go. **Wyndham Condado Plaza Hotel** (787/721-1000) boasts 402 slots, as well as 13 blackjack tables, six mini-baccarat games, and Texas hold 'em. Other 24-7 casinos in the area include **San Juan Marriott Resort** (787/722-7000) and the small **Diamond Palace Hotel and Casino** (787/721-0810). Condado is also home to **Radisson Ambassador Plaza Hotel** (787/721-7300, 10 A.M.–4 A.M.), with a whopping 489 slots.

Old San Juan has only one casino, **Sheraton Old San Juan Hotel** (787/721-5100, 8 A.M.–2 A.M.).

HORSE RACING

Just 20 minutes east of San Juan, **Hipodromo Camarero** (Carr. 3, km 15.3, Canóvanas, 787/641-6060, www.comandantepr.com, free) is a modern upscale racetrack with a restaurant, sports bar, and clubhouse with a panoramic view of the track. Races are Friday–Sunday and Wednesday, 2:30–6:30 P.M.

COCKFIGHTS

Granted, cockfighting isn't for everyone, but it is a part of Puerto Rican culture. Most cockfight arenas are in rural areas of the island, but San Juan has a large, modern, tourist-friendly facility in **Club Gallistico de Puerto Rico** (Ave. Isla

Verde at Ave. Los Gobernadores, 787/791-1557, Sat. 2–10 P.M., $5 tourists, $10 general admission). Most of the betting action takes place in the seats closest to the ring. Odds are haggled over and then bets are placed on the honor system by shouting wagers until a taker is secured. Bets are made not only on which bird will win, but on how long the fight will last. Regulars tend to be high rollers who take their bets seriously, so novices may have difficulty placing bets. Food and beer are available for purchase. This is a highly charged, testosterone-rich environment. Women are welcome, but they are advised not to dress provocatively or go alone.

Shopping

In the current era of globalization, shopping is fast becoming similarly homogenized the world over, and Puerto Rico is no different. The island is rife with large shopping malls and outlet stores selling the same designer names you could buy at Anywhere, USA. But there is also a strong culture of artisanship in Puerto Rico, and many stores sell locally made traditional crafts and contemporary artwork in varying degrees of quality. Haitian, Indonesian, and Indian import shops are plentiful too, as are high-end fine-jewelry stores. And thanks to Condado, San Juan is the place to go for high-end fashion, including Louis Vuitton and Cartier.

OLD SAN JUAN

People love to shop in Old San Juan because it offers the widest variety of unique shopping options in one pedestrian-friendly place. This is the place to go for fine jewelry, imported clothing and furnishings, cigars, folk art, tourist trinkets, and American chain stores, such as Marshalls, Walgreens, and Radio Shack.

Arts and Crafts

For visitors seeking high-quality crafts by local artisans, **Puerto Rican Arts and Crafts** (204 Calle Fortaleza, 787/725-5596, daily 9:30 A.M.–6 P.M.) is your one-stop shopping spot. This large two-level store has everything from original paintings and prints to ceramics, sculpture, jewelry, and more.

For a small selection of authentic Caribbean crafts, stop by **Tienda de Artesanías** (Museo de Las Americas in Ballajá Barracks, on Calle Norzagaray beside Quincentennial Plaza, 787/722-6057, Tues.–Fri. 10 A.M.–4 P.M., Sat.–Sun. 11 A.M.–5 P.M.). It has a nice but small mix of quality baskets, shawls, pottery, jewelry, Santos, art posters, and CDs.

Máscaras de Puerto Rico (La Calle, 105 Calle Fortaleza, 787/725-1306, Chilean@coqui.net, http://home.coqui.net/chilean, Mon.–Sat. 10 A.M.–6:30 P.M., Sun. 10:30 A.M.–5:30 P.M.) is a funky, narrow shop in a covered alleyway selling quality contemporary crafts, including masks and small reproductions of vintage *cartel* posters.

There are two nearly identical shops on the same street called **Haitian Gallery** (367 Calle Fortaleza, 787/721-4362; and 206 Calle Fortaleza, 787/725-0986, haitiangallery@aol.com, www.haitiangallerypr.com, daily 10 A.M.–6 P.M.). They both sell a great selection of Haitian folk art, including brightly colored primitive-style paintings and tons of woodwork, from sublime bowls to ornately sculpted furniture. There's a small selection of Indonesian imports, such as leaf-covered picture frames and photo albums, and tourist trinkets.

Puerto Rico Homemade Crafts Gallery (403 Calle San Francisco, 787/724-3840, http://tallercocuyopr.com, Mon.–Sat. 10:30 A.M.–8 P.M., Sun. 10:30 A.M.–6 P.M.) is an excellent source for authentic local crafts and folk art—both traditional and contemporary. The shop carries a large selection of *vejigante* masks, plus native Taíno reproductions, *cartel* posters, coconut-shell tea sets, jewelry, and Santos.

The Poets Passage (203 Calle Cruz, 787/567-9275, daily 10 A.M.–6 P.M.) offers a funky collection of local arts, crafts, and books. The store is owned by local poet and publisher Lady Lee Andrews. Poetry nights are held every Tuesday at 7 P.M.

Tourist tchotchkes, shell jewelry, *vejigante* masks, gourds, beaded necklaces, and seed jewelry can be found at **Ezense** (353 Calle Fortaleza, 787/725-1782, ezense@yahoo.com, daily 10 A.M.–7 P.M.).

Cigars

Like Cuba, Puerto Rico has a long history of hand-rolled cigar-making, and you can often find a street vendor rolling and selling his own in Plaza de Hostos's Mercado de Artesanías, a plaza near the cruise-ship piers at Calle Recinto Sur. There are also several good cigar shops selling anything you could want—except Cubans, of course. The biggest selection has to be at **The Cigar House** (255 Calle Fortaleza, 787/723-5223; 258 Calle Fortaleza, 787/725-9604; and 253 Calle San Justo, 787/725-0652; www.thecigarhousepr. com, daily 10 A.M.–6 P.M.). Trinidad, Monte Cristo, Padron 1926 and 1964, Cohiba, Perdomo, Macanudo, Partagas, Romeo and Julieta, and Puerto Rican cigars aged in rum are among those sold. They also sell tons of tourist trinkets.

For a more intimate setting, visit **El Galpón** (154 Calle del Cristo, 787/725-3945 or 888/842-5766, daily 10 A.M.–6 P.M.). This small selective shop sells a variety of quality cigars, Panama hats, masks, art prints, and superb vintage and contemporary Santos.

Imports

San Juan has several Indonesian import shops. **Eclectica** (204 Calle O'Donnell, Plaza de Colón, and 205 Calle de la Cruz, 787/721-7236 or 787/725-3163, www.eclectikasanjuan .com, daily 10 A.M.–7 P.M.) has Indonesian imports specializing in home decor, purses, and jewelry.

Hecho a Mano (260 Calle San Francisco, 787/722-0203, and 250 Calle San José,

787/725-3992, fax 787/723-0880, hechom@ coqui.net) sells Indonesian decorative imports, locally designed women's wear, funky purses, and jewelry. There's another location at 1126 Avenida Ashford in Condado.

Kamel International Bazaar and Art Gallery (154–156 Calle de la Cristo, 787/722-1455 or 787/977-7659, kamelimports@yahoo. com, daily 10:30 A.M.–6 P.M.) sells inexpensive Indian clothing, jewelry, rugs, beaded handbags, and reproduction paintings on canvas.

Surf Shop

Costazul (264 Calle San Francisco, 787/722-0991 or 787/724-8085, fax 787/725-1097, sferco@caribe.net, Mon.–Sat. 9 A.M.–7 P.M.) sells a great selection of surf and skate wear for men and women, including Oakley sunglasses and clothes by Billabong and Quiksilver. During surf season, it also stocks boards and related gear.

Fine Jewelry

There are dozens of high-end fine-jewelry stores in Old San Juan, especially along Calle Fortaleza, including **N. Barquet Joyers** (201 Calle Fortaleza, 787/721-3366 or 787/721-4051, fax 787/721-4051, nbarquet@spiderlink. net, daily 10 A.M.–5 P.M.); **Casa Diamante** (252 Calle Fortaleza, 787/977-5555, daily 10 A.M.–6 P.M.); and **Emerald Isles** (105 Calle Fortaleza, 787/977-3769, Mon.–Sat. 11 A.M.–6 P.M.).

Vogue Bazaar (364 Calle San Francisco, 787/722-1100, Mon.–Wed. and Fri.–Sat. 10 A.M.–6:30 P.M. specializes in pre-Columbian reproductions, gemstones from South America, and purses from Thailand.

Used Records and Collectibles

Thrift-store shoppers and collectors of vinyl will love **Frank's Thrift Store** (363 Calle San Francisco, 787/722-0691, daily 10 A.M.–6 P.M.). Come here to peruse the enormous used-record collection, from '80s kitsch to fresh electronica. There's even a turntable available, so you can listen to the stock before you buy. But this cluttered labyrinth of rooms is also packed with the widest assortment of junk and collectibles you could ever imagine. Decorative items, old photographs, dishes, toys, clothes—you name it.

Kitchen Goods

Spicy Caribbee (154 Calle de la Cristo, 888/725-7529, www.spicycaribbee.com, Mon.–Sat. 10 A.M.–7 P.M., Sun. 11 A.M.–5 P.M.) sells Caribbean sauces, spice mixes, coffees, soaps, fragrances, candles, cookbooks, and more.

CONDADO

Except for a few trinket sellers, most of the shopping in Condado is high-end clothing, accessories, and furnishings in the center of the neighborhood along Avenida Ashford.

Designer Clothes and Furnishings

For a fantastic variety of modern pop furniture and housewares, as well as museum-quality collectibles, go to **Articulos** (1300 Ave. Ashford, 787/723-3950, fax 787/722-5667, Mon.–Sat. 10 A.M.–6 P.M., Sun. 11 A.M.–5 P.M.). This is the place to go for monochromatic molded plastic furnishings and home decor by Alessi and Kartell. There are also great light fixtures, kitchenware, and a large selection of international bath and skin-care products. Check out the corner glass cabinet containing the highly collectible designs of Yoshitomo Nara and Marcel Dzama.

For one-of-a-kind designs, visit the eponymous store of one of the island's most renowned designers of casual wear and haute couture for both men and women, **Nono Maldonado** (1051 Ave. Ashford, 787/721-0456, 10 A.M.–6 P.M., 11 A.M.–5 P.M.). He was the former fashion editor of *Esquire* magazine.

Monsieur (1126 Ave. Ashford, 787/722-0918, Mon.–Sat. 10 A.M.–6 P.M.) sells casual designer menswear for the young and clubby.

Trendy Clothes

For something completely different, **HipHop** (1124 Ave. Ashford, 787/722-6081, Mon.–Sat. 10 A.M.–7 P.M., Sun. noon–5 P.M.) sells trendy teen wear for girls, plus Vans shoes and Kiplinger luggage.

Indonesian imports and locally designed women's wear are available at **Hecho a Mano** (1126 Ave. Ashford, 787/722-5322, fax 787/723-0880, hechom@coqui.net, Mon.–Wed. 10 A.M.–7 P.M., Thurs.–Sat. 10:30 A.M.–8 P.M., Sun. 11 A.M.–6 P.M.). It also has two locations in Old San Juan at 260 Calle San Francisco and 250 Calle San José.

Vintage Clothes

Fans of quality vintage clothing must beat a path to owner Jose Quinones' eclectic boutique, **Rockabilly** (53 Calle Barranquitas, 787/725-4665, Tues.–Sat. 10 A.M.–5 P.M.). We're talking about classic pieces by Chanel and Halston here, not to mention vintage prom dresses, stilettos, platforms, and purses. There are new vintage-inspired clothing styles too. In the back is a hair salon.

Accommodations

In addition to an enormous array of hotels, inns, and guesthouses offering every kind of accommodation imaginable, San Juan has a variety of daily, weekly, and monthly apartment rentals available to those seeking a homier or long-term place to stay. **El Viejo Adoquin** (6 Calle de la Cruz, Old San Juan, 787/977-3287, reservations@stayinpr.com, www.stayinpr.com) offers several superbly located and decorated apartments in Old San Juan, as well as one in Rincón. **The Caleta Realty** (151 Calle Clara Lair, 787/725-5347, fax 787/977-5642, reservations@thecaleta.com, www.thecaleta.com) also has many properties in Old San Juan and Condado.

OLD SAN JUAN

Aside from a large, fairly new Sheraton and a recently renovated Howard Johnson, there are

SAN JUAN

GAY PUERTO RICO

Long before Columbus arrived in Puerto Rico, native Taíno men used to beseech the moon to send them wives with a ceremonial dance in which they wore female garb. Legend has it that when the colonists witnessed the ritual, they assumed the men were homosexuals and sicced their dogs on them.

Boy, would the colonists be shocked today. Today Puerto Rico has an active, out, and proud gay community, and it is a popular destination for gay travelers. Although homosexual acts are illegal in Puerto Rico, the law is rarely if ever enforced, and there are plenty of accommodations, nightclubs, and beaches that cater to the LGBT traveler.

The island's largest gay community is in San Juan, and that's where you'll find the biggest concentration of businesses that specialize in serving gay clientele.

Accommodations popular with gay and lesbian travelers include the laid-back Ocean Park properties and **Numero Uno Guest House** (1 Santa Ana, 787/726-5010 or 866/726-5010, fax 787/727-5482, info@numero1guesthouse.com, www.numero1guesthouse.com, $143-287 s, $277-287 suite, plus $25 per additional guest, plus 9 percent tax and 15 percent service charge, children under 12 stay with parents for free), as well as the more party-central **Atlantic Beach Hotel** (1 Calle Vendig, 787/721-6900, fax 787/721-6917, www.atlanticbeachhotel.com, $115-149 s/d) in Condado. The beaches in front of these properties are the most popular gay beaches, although everyone is welcome.

There's no shortage of gay and lesbian nightclubs in San Juan. Most of the gay bars can be found in Santurce. **Atlantic Beach Bar** (1 Calle Vendig, Condado, 787/721-6900) is a casual bar at the Atlantic Beach House hotel right on the ocean, offering happy hour 5-7 P.M. **Krash** (1257 Ave. Ponce de León, 787/722-1131, www.krashpr.com, Wed.-Sat. 10 P.M.-3 A.M., $6 after midnight), formerly Eros, is a popular party spot. Wednesday is urban pop night with three DJs spinning R&B, hip-hop, and reggaetón. Thursday and Friday nights feature DJs spinning house, tribal, and retro.

In Condado, fans of salsa, reggae, and pop music flock to **Junior's** (615 Calle Condado, 787/723-9477, daily 8 P.M.-late, no cover). And in Old San Juan, **Club Le Cirque** (357 Calle San Francisco, 787/725-3246, Wed.-Sat. 6 P.M.-4 A.M.) is a gay bar and lounge with a patio that also serves lunch and dinner.

Catering to the lesbian crowd is **Cups** (1708 Calle San Mateo, Santurce, 787/268-3570, Wed.-Fri. 7 P.M.-3 A.M., Sat. 8 P.M.-3 A.M.), a laid-back spot for karaoke, live music, dance music, and a game of pool.

---

a handful of small independent hotels and inns in Old San Juan that tend to book up quickly. No matter where you stay in Old San Juan, you're within easy walking distance to some of the city's finest restaurants, shops, and cultural sights. It's worth booking ahead to stay in Old San Juan.

$100-150

By far the hippest new place to stay in San Juan, **Da House** (312 Calle San Francisco, 787/366-5074 or 787/977-1180, fax 787/725-3436, www.dahousehotelpr.com, $80–120 s/d) is owned and operated by the folks behind one of the city's hottest music clubs, Café Nuyorican. It's also located directly above the nightclub, making it a great spot for the late-night party crowd. Those inclined to go to bed early will no doubt be kept awake by the club downstairs, which doesn't close until 3 or 4 in the morning. But night owls looking to stay in elegant but casual surroundings on a student's budget would be hard-pressed to find a better hotel. The 27 units are small and sparsely furnished with just the basics—bed, lamp, mini-fridge, ceiling fan, and remote-control air-conditioning. There is no TV or phone, and fresh linens, irons, and hair dryers are available only upon request. And there's no elevator, so be prepared to walk up as many as four flights to your room—carrying your own luggage. Service is minimal—the pierced and tattooed set that runs the reception desk often do double duty in the bar downstairs. So what makes Da House so great? Besides the inexpensive rates and location in the heart of Old San Juan, it is a gorgeous building filled with fantastic contemporary art exhibitions that change every month.

When it comes to bang for the buck, you can't do much better than **(** **Hotel Milano** (307 Calle Fortaleza, 787/729-9050 or 877/729-9050, fax 787/722-3379, hmilano@ coqui.net, www.hotelmilanopr.com, $95–185 s/d plus 9 percent tax). Here you get all the modern amenities you could want but in a historic setting ideally situated among many of Old San Juan's most popular restaurants and shops. Thirty clean corporate-style rooms come with new furnishings, air-conditioning, satellite TV, hair dryers, and mini-refrigerators. An added bonus is the serviceable rooftop restaurant and bar, which provide fantastic views of the city and harbor.

Ideally located in the heart of Old San Juan on Plaza de Armas, **Hotel Plaza de Armas** (202 Calle San Jose, 787/722-9191, fax 787/725-3091, plazadearmas@hotmail.com, www.hojopr.com, $109 s, $169–179 d, $185 suites) is a simple modern hotel in a historic building renovated in 2005. The Howard Johnson property has 50 units, which comes with air-conditioning, satellite TV, and Wi-Fi. Suites come with balconies and small refrigerators; king suites sleep up to five people and have DVD players. Free continental breakfast.

$150-250

On the edge of Old San Juan overlooking the Atlantic Ocean is **The Gallery Inn** (204–206 Calle Norzagaray, 787/722-1808, fax 787/724-7360, reservations@thegalleryinn.com, www.the galleryinn.com, $175–350 s/d, plus 18 percent tax and tariff, includes breakfast buffet), one of the unique hotels in San Juan. This 18th-century home is packed with 22 small rooms tucked into a multilevel labyrinth of patios, courtyards, balconies, archways, fountains, and interior gardens. As if that weren't enough, the hotel is chock-full of portrait

sculptures and plaster reliefs by artist-owner Jan D'Esopo, as well as potted plants, hanging baskets, and an assortment of tropical birds, which have the run of the place. If the chockablock decor begins to feel a bit claustrophobic, there's an elegant, airy music room with a grand piano and a rooftop deck for a change of scenery. Small rooms are well appointed with quality antiques and reproductions. Each comes with air-conditioning and a telephone.

Nearby is the equally modern, corporate-style **SJ Suites** (253 Calle Fortaleza, 787/977-4873, 787/977-4873, or 787/725-1351, fax 787/977-7682, sjsuites@hotmail.com, www.sjsuites.com, $130–300 s/d, plus 9 percent tax, includes continental breakfast). Fifteen spanking-new, self-serve suites come with air-conditioning, satellite TV, and mini-refrigerators. There's no reception desk or on-site management. Check-in is inside Kury Jewelry Store next door.

Over $250

(**Cervantes Chateau** (329 Recinto Sur, 787/724-7722, fax 787/289-8909, reservations@cervantespr.com, www.cervantespr.com, $225 s/d, $285 junior suite, $425 suite, $975 split-level penthouse suite, plus taxes and resort fees) is a new luxury boutique hotel near the piers in Old San Juan. Tastefully but playfully decorated by clothing designer and former fashion editor at *Esquire* magazine Nono Maldonado, the hotel combines mid-century modern elements with Spanish colonial style. The emphasis is on luxury, apparent in the Egyptian linens, HDTV flat-screen TVs, and free wireless Internet. The fine dining restaurant, Panza, is on-site.

To get a true sense of history, spend the night in a Carmelite convent completed in 1651 by order of King Phillip IV of Spain. **Hotel El Convento** (100 Calle Cristo, 787/723-9020, 787/721-2877, or 800/468-2779, elconvento@ aol.com, www.elconvento.com, $325–445 s/d, $710–1,520 suite, plus taxes and resort fees). A recipient of many awards and accolades, the 58-room hotel encompasses a four-floor colonial

SAN JUAN

structure with an enormous well-landscaped courtyard in the center. Common areas are filled with gorgeous Spanish antiques and reproductions. Rooms come with air-conditioning, cable TV, VCR, stereo, telephone, and refrigerator. Amenities include a fitness center, plunge pool, and whirlpool bath on the fourth floor, which overlooks Old San Juan and the bay. It has four restaurants.

Apartment Rentals

If you want make like a local and live in a residential setting, **(Caleta Balcony Rentals** (11 Caleta de las Monjas, 787/725-5347, fax 787/977-5642, reservations@thecaleta. com, www.thecaleta.com/guesthouse.html, $80–150) offers six cozy, modest units varying from studios to one-bedroom apartments in a three-story structure near the San Juan Gate. The property is a bit shabby, but it has a great location between Hotel El Convento and La Fortaleza, home of the governor. All apartments have balconies and a full kitchen or kitchenette; some have air-conditioning, TV, and telephones. Each room is different, and they all have character to spare, but the Sunshine Suite on the third floor is the best of the bunch. There's no reception desk or on-site management at this self-serve property.

PUERTA DE TIERRA
$150-250

Puerta de Tierra is a small bit of land between Condado and Old San Juan, just west of the bridge that connects those two communities. It includes a couple of small beaches, a very large park, and a commercial district of little interest to visitors. But it does contain one amazing hotel.

When you first see the **(Normandie Hotel** (499 W. Ave. Muñoz Rivera, 787/729-2929 or 877/987-2929, www.normandiepr.com, $219–239 s/d, plus 9 percent tax) you might think you're seeing things. The 1940s art deco hotel was built to look like a grand ocean liner complete with porthole windows. Even more remarkable, the Normandie has operated continuously as an independent hotel since its

inception. Although it has seen shabbier times, it has recently been renovated with a hip eye toward minimalism. Decked out in cool shades of pale blues and greens, it's appointed with a circular porthole motif tastefully repeated in the carpets, lighting, and mirrors. There are 175 rooms, all with air-conditioning, cable TV, room safe, CD stereo system, mini-refrigerator, high-speed Internet, and concierge service. The property also has an atrium bar, an Italian restaurant, pool, beach access, spa, hair salon, and fitness center. Be sure to have a drink in the clever N Lounge, which looks like the coolest captain's quarters you've ever seen.

CONDADO
$100-150

Acacia Boutique Hotel (8 Calle Taft, 787/725-0668, 787/727-0626, or 877/725-0668, fax 787/268-2803, www.acaciaseaside inn.com, $105 s, $175–210 d) is a small, newish beachfront property from the folks at nearby Wind Chimes. Modern, modest rooms have air-conditioning and basic cable TV; some have balconies. Wireless Internet is available in common areas. Guests can use the bar and pool at Wind Chimes.

The pink oceanfront **Atlantic Beach Hotel** (1 Calle Vendig, 787/721-6900, fax 787/721-6917, www.atlanticbeachhotel.com, $115–149 s/d) serves a primarily gay clientele, but everyone is warmly welcomed. The exterior and lobby are a bit shabby, as are some of the 37 rooms, but there are some newly remodeled rooms that are more modern and comfortable. Each room has air-conditioning, satellite TV, and telephone. It has a rooftop terrace, a casual restaurant serving breakfast and lunch, and a popular ocean-side bar (happy hour 5–7 P.M.). On Sunday nights the bar hosts the Black Cat drag show. It starts at 9 P.M., but things don't really get going until around midnight.

It's at the far eastern end of Condado, several blocks from the nearest restaurant or shop, but **At Wind Chimes Inn** (1750 Ave. McLeary, 787/727-4159, fax 787/728-0671, reservations@atwindchimesinn.com, www .atwindchimesinn.com, $80–95 s, $109–150 d,

$155 suite) is just a block from the beach. Two Spanish-style haciendas have been combined to create a quaint, artful, 22-room boutique hotel. Each room has air-conditioning, cable TV, telephone, and wireless Internet; some rooms have kitchenettes. Rooms are tastefully decorated with high-quality furnishings and bright cheery bedspreads. Amenities include a small pool with jets and a waterfall, and a shady courtyard bar and grill.

Although it's about three blocks from the beach, **El Prado Inn** (1350 Calle Luchetti, 787/728-5925 or 800/468-4521, elpradoinn@ prtc.net, www.elpradoinn.net, $89–139 s/d, plus 9 percent tax and 6 percent service charge) has the benefit of being close to all the action on Avenida Ashford but with the quiet residential feel of Ocean Park. Each room is different, but they're all pleasant and comfortably decorated with a bohemian vibe. A modest continental breakfast is included, and there's a tiny pool in the courtyard. Another bonus is the lovely shaded Parque Luchetti across the street. Free parking.

The three **Canario** (800/533-2649, canario PR@aol.com, www.canariohotels.com) hotels in Condado offer small, clean, modern, no-frills accommodations at a budget rate. Rooms all come with air-conditioning, telephones, cable TV, and room safes. Service is minimal, continental breakfast is included, and all three properties are within walking distance of the beach, restaurants, shops, and bars. The one with the most attractive entrance and lobby is **El Canario Inn** (1317 Ave. Ashford, 787/722-3861, fax 787/722-0391, $115 s, $129–144 d, $144 t, $159 q, plus 9 percent tax and $5 in surcharges). Dramatic black-and-white floors and lots of plants provide a cheery welcome to its 25 units. **El Canario by the Sea** (4 Ave. Condado, 787/722-8640, fax 787/725-4921, $115 s, $129–144 d, $144 t, $159 q, plus 9 percent tax and $5 in surcharges) has 25 unremarkable rooms, a dull lobby, and lax service, but it's a mere half block from the beach. The largest property is **El Canario by the Lagoon** (4 Clemenceau, 787/722-5058, fax 787/723-8590, $119 s, $130–145 d, $145

t, $160 q, $150–180 penthouse suite, plus 9 percent tax and $5 surcharges), with 44 small basic rooms in a high-rise building beside Laguna del Condado. Rooms have balconies, and there's free parking on-site.

Over $200

(Caribe Hilton (1 Calle San Geronimo, 787/721-0303, fax 787/725-8849, sjnhi_sales@ hilton.com, www.hiltoncaribbean.com, $319 s/d, $845 one-bedroom villa, $1,216 two-bedroom villa, includes 12 percent resort tax) is proof that all Hilton hotels are not all alike. This stunning display of modernist architecture and design is a beloved blast from the past, a reminder of a time when the Condado was an epicenter of glamour. Built in the late 1940s, the sprawling hotel features an enormous lobby awash in curved lines and modular shapes that merge elegantly with blond woods, polished steel, and thick glass. Be sure to gaze up at the ceiling, a stunning wooden structure that mimics the swooping shape of ocean waves. There are seemingly countless bars, including a swim-up bar at the pool. The Caribe Hilton is one of two places in Puerto Rico (the other being Barranchina in Old San Juan) that claims to have invented the piña colada, so tourists often stop by to have one, whether they're staying at the hotel or not. And don't miss the hard-to-find Tropical Garden. Tucked away in a quiet corner is an oasis of lushly landscaped grounds built around a pond and gazebo where peacocks, geese, and black swans roam freely. There are 814 units in the hotel and nine restaurants, including Morton's the SteakHouse. There is also a spa and boutiques for shopping. Although the hotel is on the ocean, the only swimmable beach is a small public facility beside the hotel.

(Condado Plaza Hotel & Casino (999 Ave. Ashford, 787/721-1000 or 866/316-8934, www.condadoplaza.com, $199–259 s/d, $329–459 suites, plus taxes and resort fees) is an interesting bookend to the 1940s-era modernism of the Caribe Hilton. The Condado Plaza Hotel is a 21st-century modernist's dream with a minimalist aesthetic and a tastefully rendered nod to pop art sensibilities. The lobby is blindingly white with occasional touches of brilliant orange that draw the eye around the room, from the low-backed couches to the textured wooden wall treatments to the private nooks and crannies tucked behind beaded curtains. Modernist touches continue in the guest rooms, where billboard-size black-and-white photographs hang over the beds and the shower is a clear glass cube situated in the center of the spacious bathroom. The casino is open 24 hours a day, and there are multiple restaurants, including Tony Roma's and the dramatic Strip House, a steakhouse done up in red and black and appointed with black-and-white photographs of 1950s-era burlesque dancers. There is also a fitness center, a business center, and two pools, one of which is filled with salt water.

La Concha Renaissance Resort (1077 Ave. Ashford, 787/721-85000, fax 240/724-7929, www.laconcharesort.com, $309–369 s/d, $549 one-bedroom suite, plus tax and fees) was built in 1958 and is another huge, shimmering modernist hotel on the Condado. It closed and lay dormant for years, but a recent renovation has returned it to its former glory and beyond. Amenities include multilevel swimming pools with waterfalls and a sandy beach with food and beverage service, two lounges, and four restaurants, including Perla, an upscale restaurant serving contemporary American cuisine heavy on seafood in a stunning clamshell-shaped space right on the beach.

OCEAN PARK

Ocean Park boasts one of the better beaches in the metro area and some small, charming, gay-friendly guesthouses that pay a lot of attention to the kinds of details that can make an overnight stay memorable. Because this is primarily a residential neighborhood, there aren't a lot of restaurants, bars, or shops within walking distance. Also note that if you have a rental car, street parking can be scarce, especially on the weekends when locals flock to the beaches.

$100-150

You know you're in for something unique as soon as you pass the tall contemporary waterfall and koi pond at the entrance to **Hostería del Mar** (1 Calle Tapia, 787/727-3302, fax 787/727-0631 or 787/268-0772, hosteria@caribe.net, www.hosteriadelmarpr.com, $89–209 s/d, $179–239 ocean view, $244–264 suites and one-bedroom apartment, plus 9 percent tax). This compact oceanfront hotel has a lot of pizzazz in its common areas. The small lobby features an artful mix of antiques and tropical-style decor that give way to a tastefully designed Polynesian-style bar and restaurant filled with warm woods and rattan furnishings. The wooden top-hinged windows open out from the bottom, revealing the sand and sea just a few steps away. The restaurant, Uvva, specializes in what it calls Nuevo Mediterranean cuisine and serves three meals a day. The small, basic guest rooms have air-conditioning, cable TV, and telephones. A second-floor room is recommended for those sensitive to noise that sometimes emanates from the bar at night.

$150-250

Numero Uno Guest House (1 Santa Ana, 787/726-5010 or 866/726-5010, fax 787/727-5482, info@numero1guesthouse.com, www.numero1guesthouse.com, $143–287 s, $277–287 suite, plus $25 for additional guests, plus 9 percent tax and 15 percent service charge; children under 12 stay with parents for free) is a small, well-maintained guesthouse with attentive service. There's no lobby to speak of, just a tiny reception office beside a petite black-bottomed pool. But the 11 rooms are newly furnished, tastefully decorated, and comfortable, if you don't mind the compactness. Amenities include air-conditioning, a minibar, and wireless Internet. The guesthouse also boasts the popular fine-dining restaurant Pamela's, serving internationally inspired cuisine.

ISLA VERDE

When it comes to accommodations, Isla Verde is mostly home to luxury chain hotels such as the Ritz-Carlton, the Wyndham's El San Juan, and the InterContinental. But there are a handful of small independent hotels and one swanky world-class boutique hotel for the glamour set.

$100-200

If paying bottom dollar is a primary concern, you can't do much better than **Coral by the Sea** (2 Calle Rosa, 787/791-6868, fax 787/791-1672, www.coralbythesea.com, $81–103 s/d). Its small, functional, slightly dreary rooms have air-conditioning and cable TV, but it's just two blocks from the beach. Bring some air freshener, as the rooms can have a funky odor. There are two restaurants on the first floor: Platos, serving Nuevo Puerto Rican cuisine, and Piu Bello, a deli.

It may be worthwhile to pay a little more and stay at **Hotel Villa del Sol** (4 Calle Rosa, 787/791-2600 or 787/791-1600, info@villadelsolpr.com, www.villadelsolpr.com, $100 s, $130 d, $180 minisuite). In a cheerful yellow faux hacienda-style building two blocks from the beach, the inn's 24 units have air-conditioning, cable TV, and mini-refrigerators. Some rooms are starkly furnished; others are a little nicer. Amenities include a tiny pool, restaurant, bar, free parking, and free Wi-Fi in common areas. Vias Car Rental service is on-site.

Hotel La Playa (6 Calle Amapola, 787/791-1115 or 787/791-7298, reservations@hotellaplaya.com, www.hotellaplaya.com, $215 s/d with terrace, $195 ocean view, $165 standard, $125 value, plus 9 percent tax and $5 energy surcharge) is under new management and has undergone a radical renovation. What was once a shabby budget hotel is now a sophisticated, moderately priced oasis in Isla Verde. Rooms have been updated with quality contemporary furnishings, tile floors, and new fixtures in the bathrooms. The kitschy boat bar in the lobby is no more, but a new full service restaurant, La Playita, has been added, serving casual and upscale creative cuisine with vegetarian options. Plans are underway to transform the neglected rooftop terrace into an open-air spa. And a new deck offers seaside sunbathing right on the water. Amenities include air-conditioning and satellite TV.

Over $200

The South Beach party crowd gravitates to **The Water Club** (2 Calle Tartak, 787/728-3666 or 888/265-6699, fax 787/728-3610, info@waterclubsanjuan.com, www.waterclub.com, $179–399 s/d). The modern high-design boutique hotel offers super-luxurious accommodations for the young, trendy, and well-heeled crowd. The hotel's 75 rooms come with air-conditioning, satellite TV, CD players, two-line telephones, data ports, high-speed Internet, minibars, in-room safes, and superior beds topped with down comforters. Water is the theme of this stark white and aqua property: Bubbles float in Lucite countertops at the reception desk, and water features abound. Liquid, the lobby bar, has a corrugated tin wall with a constant flow of water trickling over it. Wet, the rooftop bar, features stunning views of the city and huge leather couches and beds—yes, beds—that spill out around the pool. The restaurant, Tangerine, serves American Asian cuisine.

Food

In recent years, San Juan's dining scene has experienced an evolution. More and more new restaurants have opened serving sophisticated international, Nuevo Latino, and Puerto Rican fusion cuisines in chic and trendy settings. But plenty of traditional restaurants serving authentic Puerto Rican cuisine can still be found, even in San Juan.

OLD SAN JUAN
Caribbean

The locally owned OOF! Restaurants group is in large part responsible for raising the dining standards in San Juan. The first of its four restaurants is (**The Parrot Club** (363 Calle Fortaleza, 787/725-7370, www.oofrestaurants .com, lunch Mon.–Fri. 11:30 A.M.–3 P.M., Sat.–Sun. 11:30 A.M.–4 P.M.; dinner Sun.–Wed. 6–11 P.M., Thurs.–Sat. 6 P.M.–midnight; bar Sun.–Wed. until midnight, Thurs.–Sat. until 1 A.M.; $17–32), which opened in 1996. At first glance, this wildly popular restaurant might look like a prefab tourist attraction. It boasts a Disneyesque tropical-island theme, complete with faux palm trees and wooden parrots, and the din around the crowded bar can make conversation a challenge. But the reality is the Parrot Club serves some of the island's finest interpretations of Nuevo Latino cuisine. If you prefer a nice, quiet, leisurely served meal, bypass the bar and ask to be seated in the calm low-lit courtyard out back. The restaurant specializes in a smorgasbord of crisp, refreshing seviches, featuring a wide selection of seafood marinated in fresh citrus juices and served chilled. The shrimp, *chillo* (snapper), and *dorado* (mahimahi) are the best of the bunch. If you want something a little heartier, try the thick slab of blackened tuna steak served in a dark, slightly sweet sauce of rum and orange essence. It's an addictive dish that will have you coming back for more.

A pair of kids find a snack on Calle San Sebastían in Old San Juan.

© SUZANNE VAN ATTEN

Baru (150 Calle San Sebastían, 787/977-7107 or 787/977-5442, Mon.–Sat. 6 P.M.–midnight, Sun. 5:30 P.M.–midnight, $10–28) is a lovely, sensuous restaurant with a casually elegant atmosphere that melds classic architectural features with contemporary art, and then bathes it all in warm low lighting that makes you want to linger long after your meal is over. The cuisine is a creative combination of Caribbean and Mediterranean dishes, carefully prepared and artfully presented. Serving sizes are slightly bigger than an appetizer and smaller than an entrée, so order several and share with your tablemates. For an excellent starter, go with the goat cheese and almond spread drizzled with mango sauce and served with long fried yucca chips. Its satisfying combination of creamy and crunchy textures pairs beautifully with the blend of sweet and savory flavors. The asparagus risotto is appropriately creamy and nubby on the tongue, and it's studded with just the right amount of fresh chopped stalks and tips. Plump, slightly charred scallops are served each in their own tiny shell-shaped dish, drizzled with a delicate coconut curry sauce, and flecked with fresh mint. But skip the pork ribs. Although falling-off-the-bone tender, they're slathered in a supersweet guava sauce that overwhelms the flavor of the meat.

The atmospheric **El Asador Grill** (350 Calle San Francisco, 787/289-0489, Sun.–Thurs. 11 A.M.–midnight, Fri–Sat. 11 A.M.–4 A.M., $13–37.50), located in a contemporary faux hacienda-style setting, specializes in grilled meats prepared in a courtyard kitchen. Cream-colored stucco walls, dark wood beams, terra-cotta tile floors, and dramatic archways create an inviting environment. And the menu is a carnivore's delight. Beyond the usual grilled steak, chicken, pork, and fish, you can get sausages, sweetbreads, and kidney too. Unfortunately the service was consistently abysmal on repeated visits. If the staff were more professional and welcoming, this place would come highly recommended.

Puerto Rican

Although it might seem like it at first glance, trendy upscale restaurants are not the only options in Old San Juan for traditional Puerto Rican cuisine. Fairly new on the scene is **Restaurante Raices** (315 Calle Recinto Sur, 787/289-2121, www.restauranteraices.com, daily 11 A.M.–11 P.M., $10–29), a casual, moderately priced spot for expertly prepared traditional Puerto Rican cuisine. Specialties include *mofongo* stuffed with *chimichurri* and mahimahi stuffed with shrimp. The original location is in Caguas.

Despite the dreadful service, **La Fonda El Jibarito** (280 Calle Sol, 787/725-8375, daily 11 A.M.–9 P.M., $5.50–18) is one of the best bets for authentic Puerto Rican cuisine, including codfish stew, fried pork, fried snapper, great rice and beans, and *mofongo*, cooked and mashed plantain seasoned with garlic. It's a major staple. Sometimes it's stuffed with meat or seafood. Patrons share tables in this casual restaurant designed to look like a traditional country house. Between the blaring TV and many families with small children, the noise level can be overwhelming. Thank goodness there's a full bar.

Café Puerto Rico (208 Calle O'Donnell, 787/724-2281, cafepr@coqui.net, Mon.–Sat. 11:30 A.M.–4:30 P.M. and 5:30–11 P.M., Sun. 11 A.M.–9 P.M., $9–20) has a whole new lease on life. The plain little café beside Plaza Colon that was there forever and never changed a bit is no more: The place has been outfitted in rich dark wood paneling and a new tile bar with tastefully lit contemporary artwork hanging on the walls. It's quite a transformation, but the coffee is still outstanding, and the Puerto Rican cuisine is still good solid fare. You can get everything from *asopao* and *mofongo* to paella and steak.

Several historic restaurants in Old San Juan have been serving customers for more than 100 years. One of the most venerable is **La Mallorquina** (207 Calle San Justo, 787/722-3261, Mon.–Sat. noon–10 P.M., $9–36), which has been in operation since 1848. This Old World white-linen restaurant serves traditional Puerto Rican cuisine, specializing in *asopao*, a hearty traditional rice stew served with a choice of meats or seafoods.

SAN JUAN

La Bombonera (259 Calle San Franciso, 787/722-0658, fax 787/795-2175, daily 6 A.M.–8 P.M., $7.25–14.45) was established in 1902. This huge dingy diner and bakery serves a large menu of fairly pedestrian Puerto Rican fare, including rice stews and sandwiches. But the best reason to go is for its famous *mallorca*, a light flaky piece of swirled pastry split lengthwise, stuffed with butter, smashed, heated on a grill press, and dusted with powdered sugar. The crispy breakfast sandwiches are also a good hearty way to start the day. But be prepared to wait: Service is excruciatingly slow, especially when you're waiting for the morning's first cup of coffee.

(Mallorca (300 Calle San Francisco, 787/724-4607, daily 7 A.M.–7 P.M., $5.95–17.95) offers a very similar dining experience to that at La Bombonera, complete with its namesake pastry, but with friendlier, more attentive service.

Barrachina (104 Calle Fortaleza, 787/721-5852, 787/725-7912, www.barrachina.com, Tues.–Sat. 11 A.M.–10 P.M., $14–45), located in the courtyard of a 17th-century building, is one of two places in Puerto Rico (the Caribe Hilton being the other) that claims to have invented the piña colada. They mix up a pretty good one. But the budget decor was looking pretty shabby on a recent visit, and the Puerto Rican cuisine was only adequate.

New American

Prepare yourself for an unforgettable dining experience at **(Marmalade** (317 Calle Fortaleza, 787/724-3969, fax 787/724-4001, www.marmaladepr.com, Mon.–Thurs. 6–11 P.M., Fri.–Sat. 6 P.M.–midnight, Sun. 6–10 P.M., bar daily 5 P.M. until late, $24.50–29). This lovely, romantic chef-owned restaurant serves an ever-changing eclectic seasonal menu. The fun starts with the creative cocktail menu: Cointreau jelly, kiwi puree, jasmine flowers, and Compari foam were among the ingredients featured on a recent visit. Appetizers included pan-roasted foie gras and prosciutto di Parma, served with grilled peaches. Among the entrées were duck breast stuffed with Roquefort cheese and apple slices, and lamb lasagna made with Persian feta cheese. For pure drama, dine in the bar area, where great sheaths of aqua, orange, and rose-colored silk organza drape from the high ceilings to the floor and marble-top tables are surrounded by deep plush couches with curved backs loaded with pillows. The sedate dining room in the back is more quietly elegant.

Located in the luxury Chateau Cervantes boutique hotel, **Panza** (329 Recinto Sur, 787/289-8900, www.cervantespr.com, daily 8 A.M.–noon, Mon.–Sat. 6–11 P.M., $26–35), is a new fine-dining restaurant serving creative interpretations of classic dishes. The lobster bisque with coconut is a specialty.

Spanish

In the historic Hotel El Convento, the focal point of **El Picoteo** tapas and paella bar (100 Calle Cristo, 787/723-9020, 787/721-2877, or 800/468-2779, elconvento@aol.com, www.elconvento.com, daily noon–11 P.M., $7–29) is the original woodstove of the former convent, which was built in the mid-17th century. Visitors are greeted at the entrance by an enormous wax-covered altar packed willy-nilly with whimsical ceramic roosters and half-melted candles. The main dining room is in the hotel courtyard, but there's also dining at the long tile bar overlooking the open kitchen. The traditional Spanish tapas include stiff planks of Manchego cheese, thin slices of buttery serrano ham, fresh sardines, and a variety of olives. Bypass the mushy, oily eggplant and roasted red-pepper salad, but definitely order the fiery bite-size chorizo sausages served in a pool of thin heady brandy sauce. Among the varieties of paellas is one prepared with nutty, earthy black rice and chock-full of shrimp, calamari, and chunks of *dorado*.

Italian

Fratelli (310 Calle Fortaleza, 787/721-6265, fax 787/729-2238, www.restaurantefratelli.com, Mon.–Sat. 6 P.M. until the place empties, $15–30) is another terrific restaurant from the owners of Baru, this one serving Italian cuisine in a classic Old World setting featuring high ceilings, a graceful archway, potted palms, a fresco on one wall, and a ceiling-high shelf lined with bottles of wine on another. As at Baru, the artful lighting creates a sumptuous ambiance that encourages you to linger long into the night. The food is superb, especially the fresh pasta made on the premises. Specialties include seafood linguine and risotto, beef and tuna carpaccios, and a *Caprese* salad that's almost too pretty to eat. It also has a full bar and extensive wine list.

Seafood and Steak

For a hip, hot restaurant where the gorgeous wait staff is attitude-free, the seafood is amazing, and the decor is evocative of dining in an aquarium, get thee to 【 **Aguaviva** (364 Calle Fortaleza, 787/722-0665, www.oofrestaurants.com, daily 11:30 A.M.–4 P.M., Mon.–Thurs. and Sun. 6–11 P.M., Fri.–Sat. 6 P.M.–midnight, $17–30), another of the OOF! Restaurants' purveyors of contemporary cuisine. The space is drenched in bright white, chrome, and aqua, with glass jellyfish lights hanging from the ceiling. In addition to an oyster and seviche bar, dishes on a recent visit included grilled *dorado* with smoked shrimp salsa, grilled marlin with chorizo, and nueva paella with seared scallops. At the blue-lit bar, where seashells float in Lucite, sublime cocktails are prepared with fresh juices. Be sure to try the watermelon sangria.

Romance oozes from the patio of **Ostra Cosa** (154 Calle Cristo, 787/722-COSA—787/722-2672, Sun.–Wed. noon–10 P.M., Fri.–Sat. noon–11 P.M., $14–28). This lovely intimate restaurant in the back of Las Arcadas alley has just 11 tables on a red brick patio under a white tent surrounded by scores of tropical plants and orchids. The cuisine is mostly seafood, including grilled prawns, Alaskan crab legs, and cheesy crepes stuffed with your choice of fillings. For something unusual, try the smoked calamari salad, a refreshing combination of thin slices of tender pink calamari with bits of seaweed in a spritz of light ginger sauce. Accompany that with the house cocktail, the

Spinoza, a bracing mixture of white rum and fresh-squeezed lime juice. There's live mood-setting music on weekends.

Asian

Dragonfly (364 Calle Fortaleza, 787/977-3886, www.oofrestaurants.com, Mon.–Wed. 6–11 P.M., Thurs.–Sat. 6 A.M.–midnight, $12–26), another OOF! Restaurant establishment frequented by the young and beautiful party set, has recently been expanded from a tiny intimate space to encompass a lounge and second bar. Nevertheless, be prepared for the wait to get in, unless you go early in the night. The playful fusion menu offers delightfully creative cuisine combinations, such as Asian seared scallops and miso honey halibut. There's also a full-service sushi menu.

A fusion of Indian and Puerto Rican cuisine may seem an unusual combination, but 【 **Tantra** (356 Calle Fortaleza, 787/977-8141, fax 787/977-4289, www.tantrapr.com, daily noon–midnight, late-night menu Mon.–Sat. midnight–3 A.M., $16–29) proves just how simpatico the dishes are. Sensual creations include crispy fried coconut sesame shrimp accompanied by a mango-peach salsa, and shredded tandoori chicken served over a platter of crispy fried plantain slices. The menu of eclectic small plates encourages sharing. If you can't decide, order one of the combo platters that serve 2–4 diners ($55–75). The bar serves a variety of fruity martinis ($10) garnished with fresh flower petals. Forgo dessert and have a coconut martini rimmed in chocolate and fresh grated coconut instead. After dinner, fire up a bowl of fruit-flavored tobacco in one of the hookahs that line the bar ($20 a bowl). When the kitchen closes, Tantra turns into a late-night hotspot popular with service-industry workers who flock there when their restaurants close.

French

For traditional French cuisine in a classic elegant setting featuring an enormous crystal chandelier and walls surrounded by long white flowing drapes, there's **Trois**

Cent Onze (311 Calle Fortaleza, 787/725-7959, www.311restaurantpr.com, Wed.–Fri. noon–3 P.M., Tues.–Thurs. 6:30–10:30 P.M., Fri.–Sat. 6:30–11:30 P.M., $22–35). This is the place to go for snails and foie gras. Check out their highly lauded wine-pairing dinners.

Eclectic

Carli Café Concierto (Banco Popular building, corner of Recinto Sur and Calle San Justo, 787/725-4927, carli@caribe.net, www.carlicafeconcierto.com, Mon.–Sat. 11:30 A.M.–2:30 P.M., 5–10 P.M., live music Mon.–Sat. 8–11:30 P.M., $16–34) is a romantic, sophisticated lounge and restaurant serving a variety of dishes, including risottos, raviolis, quesadillas, and Caribbean-inspired tapas. The owner, a jazz pianist, performs nightly with a changing array of guest musicians. It's also a great place to just sit at the bar and enjoy one of a large selection of specialty cocktails. There's alfresco dining on the sidewalk too.

OCEAN PARK

There are few restaurants in Ocean Park, but the ones that are there are top-notch. Despite its name, **◖ Kasalta Bakery** (1966 Ave. McLeary, 787/727-7340 or 787/727-6593, fax 787/268-0864, www.kasalta.com, daily 6 A.M.–10 P.M.) is much more than a bakery. This large, professionally run operation sells piping hot *empanadillas, pastelillos,* and *alcapurrias* ($1.50), and super-thick toasted sandwiches ($4.50–8), including an exceptional Cubano, *media noche,* and a variety of breakfast sandwiches. There are also hot daily specials, including paella, seafood salads, and case after case of freshly made baked goods ($1.50) such as cheesecakes, jelly rolls, Danish, cookies, and more. It also sells whole cakes and has an excellent wine and liquor selection. Order at the counter and grab a seat on a short bar stool at shared tables to feast. Be prepared to wait for a parking space and stand in lines to order on the weekends.

In Numero Uno guesthouse, **Pamela's** (1 Calle Santa Ana, 787/726-5010, fax 787/727-5482, www.numero1guesthouse.com, lunch daily noon–3 P.M.; tapas daily 3–6 P.M.; dinner daily 6–10:30 P.M., $22–29) is the most popular restaurant in Ocean Park. This elegant fine-dining restaurant with excellent service features white linen tablecloths and mission-style furnishings inside, with casual seating outside right on the sandy beach. Specialties include grilled shrimp with tamarind sauce and rack of lamb with grilled pineapple and fresh mint chutney.

Uvva (at Hostería del Mar guesthouse, 1 Calle Tapia, 787/727-3302, fax 787/727-0631, www.hosteriadelmarpr.com, daily 8 A.M.–10 P.M., $20–36) is another popular fine-dining restaurant in Ocean Park. It features a tiny dining room decked out in warm woods and rattan furnishings. The cuisine is Mediterranean fusion, featuring several pasta dishes, fish, and lamb chops.

CONDADO
Puerto Rican

◖ Ajili-Mójili (1006 Ave. Ashford, 787/725-9195, ajiligroup@yahoo.com, Mon.–Fri. 11:45 A.M.–3 P.M., Sat. noon–3:30 P.M., Sun. buffet noon–4 P.M., Sun.–Thurs. 6–10 P.M., Fri.–Sat. 6–11 P.M., $14–29) comes highly recommended for its upscale take on traditional Puerto Rican cuisine if you don't mind the Disneyfied ambiance. The large space is tricked out like a faux colonial-style hacienda, and the wait staff wears plantation garb, including suspenders and Panama hats. Dishes include *mofongo, arroz con pollo,* plantain-breaded snapper fillets, coconut shrimp with piña colada sauce, and stuffed Cornish hen. The clubby wood and glass-tile bar is a great place to meet for cocktails.

The late-night party crowd likes **Latin Star Restaurant** (1128 Ave. Ashford, 787/724-8141, $3.95–29.95) less for the food and more for the fact that it's open 24-7. It serves a huge menu, including authentic local dishes such as goat or rabbit stew, tripe soup, and brandied guinea. There's indoor and sidewalk dining, and if you want to keep the party going, Dom Perignon is on the wine list.

Orozco's Restaurant (1126 Ave. Ashford, 787/721-7669, daily 11 A.M.–11:30 P.M., $9.95–19.95) serves traditional Puerto Rican cuisine featuring *mofongo,* grilled steak, pork, and chicken, plus daily specials. There is a full bar; try the house-made sangria.

It's rare to find a true locals' place in Condado. That's what makes **Cafe Condado** (Ashford Medical Center, Ave. Ashford, 787/722-5963, Sun.–Fri. 5:30 A.M.–5:30 P.M., Sat. 7 A.M.–2 P.M.) so appealing. Little more than a drab crowded diner, this eatery is the perfect antidote to the corporate American chain restaurants that line the eastern end of Ashford Avenue. In the back of Ashford Medical Center, it serves good cheap Puerto Rican cuisine, including *carne guisada* (beef stew) and ham croquettes ($5.50–7.25), breakfast and sandwiches ($2.25–4.75), and an excellent cup of coffee ($0.50).

Seafood

For an unforgettable fine-dining experience, visit ◖ **Perla** (La Concha Renaissance Resort, 1077 Ave. Ashford, 787/977-3285, www.perla restaurant.com, Sun.–Thurs. 6–10 P.M., Fri.–Sat. 6–11 P.M., Sun. brunch noon–3 P.M., $25–39). The architecture is reason enough to go. The restaurant is nestled inside a 1958-era modernist interpretation of a clamshell located right on the beach. The seasonal menu leans mostly toward seafood and is ever-changing, depending on the availability of the freshest ingredients. Recent selections included frog's leg skillet chowder, skate wing poached in duck fat, and fennel-dusted diver scallops.

A casual option for good local cuisine is ◖ **Marisqueria La Dorada** (1105 Ave. Magdalena, 787/722-9583, daily 11 A.M.–10 P.M., tapas $5.95–9.95, entrées $16.95–29.95). The cute, cheerful little eatery serves terrific Puerto Rican cuisine, specializing in seafood. The bite-size *piononos*—balls of sweet plantain stuffed with spicy ground beef and deep-fried—make an excellent starter. Check the board for daily specials, including codfish in passion-fruit sauce and whole fried snapper.

Ikakos Restaurante Marisqueria (1108 Ave. Ashford, 787/723-5151, www.ikakos .com, Tues. and Thurs. noon–10 P.M., Wed. and Fri. noon–10 P.M., Sat. 5–11 P.M., Sun. noon–10 P.M., $10.95–28.95) is a casual but elegantly appointed seafood restaurant specializing in fresh local lobster and whole fish. Oysters, mussels, and *empanadillas* make up the tapas menu, while entrées feature *mofongo* and *mamposteao,* a sautéed rice dish served with your choice of meat or seafood.

Waikiki Caribbean Food & Oyster Bar (1025 Ave. Ashford, 787/977-2267, daily 11 A.M.–late, $12–35), a casual oceanfront restaurant, features a long pinewood bar, sidewalk dining, a stone grotto-style dining room inside, and a wood deck on the beach for alfresco dining. Dishes include mahimahi nuggets, crab-stuffed mushrooms, lobster tail, osso buco, and seafood *criolla.*

Cuban

A trendy take on Cuban cuisine can be found at **Ropa Vieja Grill** (1025 Ave. Ashford, 787/725-2665, Sun.–Wed. 11 A.M.–10:30 P.M., Thurs. 11:30 A.M.–11 P.M., Fri. 11:30 A.M.–midnight, Sat. 6 P.M.–midnight, $15–25). A modern space with a large cherrywood bar, tile floors, and a wall of windows that provides great people-watching, the restaurant serves risotto with pork rinds, filet medallions in Roquefort sauce, and grilled sea bass in pesto sauce.

Italian

In the heart of all the high-rises in Condado is a little seaside oasis called **Barlovento** (Plaza del Ancla on Ave. Ashford, 787/724-7286, Sun.–Wed. 5–11:30 P.M., Thurs.–Sat. 5 P.M.–midnight, $12–25). In a small park, the restaurant offers outdoor dining under a modernistic pavilion with purple awnings and chrome chairs. Like its counterparts in Old San Juan, Baru and Fratelli, it serves excellently prepared but less formal Mediterranean cuisine, including grilled chorizo, eggplant *rollatina,* and a variety of creative pizzas. Full bar.

Via Appia's Deli (1350 Ave. Ashford, 787/725-8711 or 787/722-4325, daily

11 A.M.–midnight, $12–30) serves standard red-sauce Italian dishes, including pasta, sandwiches, and pizzas. It has indoor and sidewalk dining.

Spanish

Don't be put off by the drab exterior of **Urdin** (1105 Ave. Magdalena, 787/724-0420, Mon.–Fri. noon–3 P.M. and 6–10:30 P.M., Sat. 6–10:30 P.M., $17.95–27.95). Inside is a shocking contrast: an elegant, contemporary dining room filled with thick carpets and dramatic paintings. The Spanish-influenced menu features several unusual dishes, including mussel croquettes, sweetbread cakes, wild boar chops, and roast duck in sour chocolate sauce. Take advantage of the valet parking.

Across the street from Urdin is a fine classic restaurant called **Ramiro's** (1106 Ave. Magdalena, 787/721-9056 or 787/721-9049, fax 787/722-6067, ramiros@caribe.net, http://premium.caribe.net/~ramiros, Mon. noon–4 P.M., Tues.–Fri. noon–9 P.M., $13–37). In a gorgeous green Spanish colonial mansion with enormous stained-glass windows, this chef-owned restaurant has exquisite table settings and tons of Old World style. The cuisine is international with an emphasis on Spanish interpretations, including halibut with banana chutney, yellowfin tuna in snail and chorizo sauce, and osso buco lasagna with foie sauce.

Mexican

On Avenida Magdalena is a pair of Mexican restaurants with the same name, **Cielito Linda** (1108 Ave. Magdalena, 787/723-5597 or 787/723-5597). The one on the left (Mon.–Fri. 11:30 A.M.–10 P.M., Sat. 6–11 P.M., Sun. 5–10 P.M., $4.95–17.95) is a tiny kitschy taqueria serving fajitas, enchiladas, tacos, and burritos. Two doors down is a slightly bigger, nicer eatery (Thurs. 5–11 P.M., Fri.–Sat. 6–11 P.M., Sun. 5–10 P.M., $7.95–19.95) serving beef tenderloin, marinated pork, and shrimp in tequila sauce, in addition to the typical taco, enchilada, and burrito fare. Both have full bars and specialize in frozen drinks.

Hacienda Don Jose (1025 Ave. Ashford, 787/722-5880, daily 7 A.M.–11 P.M., $12.95–32.95. A casual spot serving Puerto Rican and Mexican cuisine, including tacos, enchiladas, and burritos.

SANTURCE

One of San Juan's most exclusive restaurants is ◖ **Pikayo** (Museo de Arte de Puerto Rico, 299 Ave. José de Diego, 787/721-6194, fax 787/724-8280, www.wilobenet.com, Tues.–Fri. noon–3 P.M., Mon.–Sat. 6–11 P.M., $32–70), just a few blocks south across Highway 26 from Condado. This is expense-account dining at its most lavish, and don't expect to save money by going for lunch—it's the same menu as for dinner. The seasonal menu changes, but dishes during a recent visit included octopus carpaccio and rack of lamb with shiitake mushroom stuffing. The food is superb. Reservations are recommended for dinner.

At the opposite end of the cost spectrum is **Plaza del Mercado,** at the end of Calle Roberts off Calle Canals. If the tourist scene along the Condado gets to be too predictable, venture just eight blocks inland for an authentic Puerto Rican experience. At this small historic market built in 1910, vendors sell fresh fruit, vegetables, and cut-to-order meat for far less than you'd pay at the local grocery store. You can also find herbs and roots from the *botanicas,* pick up a few sundries, and have a fresh blended fruit shake, with or without rum. Packed around the market are a number of bars and restaurants serving Puerto Rican cuisine. This is a popular place for working-class locals to congregate on Friday afternoons to get their weekends started, and the partying lasts well into the night. A convenient ATM is on Calle Roberts just before the market entrance.

ISLA VERDE
Puerto Rican

Platos Restaurant (below Coral by the Sea hotel, 2 Calle Rosa, 787/791-7474 or 787/721-0396, Sun.–Thurs. 11 A.M.–11 P.M., Fri.–Sat. 11 A.M.–midnight, $17–23) is not named after the Greek philosopher but rather the Spanish word for "plates." This trendy, touristy restaurant is decorated in moss green and burned orange with a large steel counter and big-screen TV in the bar. Tropical-drink specials are tall, but weak and pricey at $12 a pop. The formerly froufrou menu has been replaced with streamlined traditional dishes including *mofongo,* steaks, pork chops, and fettuccine. Creativity reigns among the seafood dishes, which include mahimahi in coconut–passion fruit sauce. **Casa Dante** (39 Ave. Isla Verde, 787/726-7310, Mon.–Thurs. 11:30 A.M.–1 A.M., Fri.–Sat. 11:30 A.M.–midnight, Sun. 11:30 A.M.–10:30 P.M., $8–30) is a casual, low-key locals' restaurant serving authentic Puerto Rican cuisine, specializing in a variety of *mofongos* with choice of fish, seafood, beef, chicken, or pork. There are also a few pasta dishes available.

Seafood and Steak

Locals and tourists alike flock to 【 **Che's** (corner of Calle Caoba and Calle Laurel, 787/726-7202 or 787/268-7507, Sun.–Thurs. noon–11 P.M., Fri.–Sat. noon–midnight, $12.95–28.95), a large casual restaurant serving excellent Argentine cuisine. Grilled meats are the specialty—veal, lamb, *churrasco,* veal kidneys, and so on. There are also some unexpected offerings—a Greek-style spinach pie with a whole boiled egg buried inside and an apple and celery salad. Che's has good service and a full bar.

Cuban

Decor is secondary at the crowded casual Cuban restaurant 【 **Metropol** (Ave. Isla Verde, beside Club Gallistico cockfight arena, 787/791-4046, www.metropolpr.com, daily 11:30 A.M.–10:30 P.M., $8.95–34.95, although most dishes are $10–15). The house specialty is *gallinita rellena de congri*—succulent roasted Cornish hen stuffed with a perfectly seasoned combination of rice and black beans. The presentation is no-nonsense and the service expedient, designed to get you in and out so the folks lining up outside can have your table.

Italian

Despite its modest location on the busy thoroughfare, **Il Nonno** (41 Ave. Isla Verde, 787/728-8050, Sun.–Thurs. 11:30 A.M.–10 P.M., Fri.–Sat. 11:30 A.M.–11 P.M., $14–29) is a small fine-dining restaurant with a lovely setting. Pale green walls and walnut accents are complemented by an excellent selection of contemporary paintings. The restaurant serves Italian cuisine from gnocchi Gorgonzola to osso buco.

The casual modern Argentine-Italian restaurant **Ferrari Gourmet** (51 Ave. Isla Verde, 787/982-3115, Ferrari@caribe.net, Sun.–Thurs. noon–10 P.M., Fri.–Sat. noon–11 P.M., delivery after 6 P.M., $9.95–21.95) specializes in a wide variety of tasty creative pizzas. Selections include black olive and blue cheese; asparagus, parmesan cheese, and fresh tomato; and ham, roasted red peppers, and green olives. Entrées include *churrasco,* veal saltimbocca, and lasagna.

Deli

Piu Bello (2 Calle Rosa, 787/791-0091, fax 787/791-0092, Mon.–Thurs. 7 A.M.–11 P.M., Fri.–Sun. 7 A.M.–midnight, $6.99–12.99) is a large, modern retro-style diner with indoor and outdoor dining. The enormous menu includes every sandwich imaginable, including wraps, Italian focaccias, flatbreads, paninis, burgers, and clubs. It also serves breakfast, pasta dishes, and gelato. A second location is on Avenida Ashford in Condado. There's free Wi-Fi.

Information and Services

TOURIST INFORMATION

Puerto Rico Tourism Company (La Casita, Plaza de la Dársena, Old San Juan, 787/722-1709, fax 787/722-5208, www.goto puertorico.com, Sat.–Wed. 8:30 A.M.–8 P.M., Thurs.–Fri. 8:30 A.M.–6:30 P.M.) is in a small yellow colonial building near San Juan Bay, conveniently located near the cruise ship piers. It's a good place to pick up promotional brochures on various tourist sites, hotels, and tours, as well as a free rum cocktail.

Tourism Office of San Juan (250 Calle Teután at Calle San Justo, Old San Juan, 787/721-6363, Mon.–Sat. 8 A.M.–4 P.M.) offers self-guided audio tours of Old San Juan in English and Spanish for $9.99 per person. There's also a random selection of promotional materials for local tourist sites, hotels, and tours.

NEWSPAPERS AND MAGAZINES

El Nuevo Día (www.endi.com) is the island-wide Spanish-language daily newspaper.

There are two English-language travel magazines devoted to Puerto Rico. The free bimonthly *Qué Pasa?* (www.qpsm.com) is published by Travel and Sports (www.travel andsports.com) for the Puerto Rico Tourism Company. The magazine's current issue is available online, and the publishing company's website is an exhaustive source of information about the entire island. *Travel and Tourism Puerto Rico* is a quarterly publication available for purchase at magazine stands. Both are good sources for general tourist information, but they tend to be promotional and not very subjective.

EMERGENCY SERVICES

The central hospital serving San Juan's tourist areas is **Ashford Medical Center** (1451 Ave. Ashford, Condado, 787/721-2160). The clinic is open Monday–Friday 7 A.M.–7 P.M., Saturday 7 A.M.–noon. The emergency room is open 24 hours a day. Call 911 for ambulance service. There's a pharmacy on the first floor.

There are several **Walgreens** pharmacies (201 Calle de la Cruz at Calle San Francisco, Old San Juan, 787/722-6290; 1130 Ave. Ashford, Condado, 787/725-1510; 5984 Ave. Isla Verde, Isla Verde, 787/982-0222). Another option is **Puerto Rico Pharmacy** (157 Calle San Francisco, Old San Juan, 787/725-2202).

Dial 911 to reach the fire or police departments in case of emergency.

OTHER SERVICES

There is no shortage of banks and ATMs in San Juan, the most popular being **Banco Popular** (206 Calle Tetuán, Old San Juan, 787/725-2636; 1060 Ave. Ashford, Condado, 787/725-4197; 4790 Ave. Isla Verde, Isla Verde, 787/726-5600).

Convenient **post office** facilities are at 153 Calle Fortaleza, Old San Juan, 787/723-1277; and 1108 Calle Magdalena, Condado, 787/723-8204.

Self-service laundries are available at **Coin Laundry** (1950 Calle Magdalena, Condado, 787/726-5955) and **Isla Verde Laundromat** (corner of Calle Emma and Calle Rodríguez, Isla Verde, 787/728-5990).

Getting There and Getting Around

GETTING THERE
By Air

Aeropuerto Internacional Luis Muñoz Marín (SJU, Isla Verde, 787/791-4670 or 787/791-3840, fax 787/253-3185 or 787/791-4834) is nine miles east of San Juan. It is a full-service airport with three terminals. There are a bank, restaurants, bars, and shops on the second floor alongside the departure gates. A tourist-information office (787/791-1014) is in Terminal C, and a ground-service desk is on the first level by the baggage claim.

For transportation into the city from the airport, there are several car-rental agencies on the first level, including **Wheelchair Getaway Rent A Car** (787/726-4023), which provides vehicles for drivers with disabilities. The first level is also where you can catch a taxi or bus into town. From the airport, take Baldorioty de Castro Avenue west toward Isla Verde, Ocean Park, and Condado and into Old San Juan.

The airport also is the site of the Luis Muñoz Marín International Airport Hotel (787/791-1700), which can be found in Terminal D on the second level.

Airline ticket prices fluctuate throughout the year, but the cheapest rates can usually be secured during the off-season, May–September, which is the rainy season. Note that late summer and early fall are also hurricane season.

The following airlines service San Juan from the United States:

- **AirTran** (800/247-8726, www.airtran.com)
- **American Airlines** (800/433-7300, www.aa.com)
- **Continental Airlines** (800/231-0856 or 800/523-3273, www.continental.com)
- **Delta Air Lines** (800/221-1212 or 800/325-1999, www.delta.com)
- **JetBlue Airways** (800/538-2583, www.jetblue.com)
- **Northwest** (800/225-2525, www.nwa.com)
- **Spirit Airlines** (800/772-7117, www.spiritairlines.com)
- **United** (800/864-8331, www.united.com)
- **U.S. Airways** (800/428-4322, www.usairways.com)

Aeropuerto de Isla Grande (End of Ave. Lindberg, Puerta de Tierra near Old San Juan, 787/729-8790, fax 787/729-8751) is a regional airport that services flights throughout the island and the Caribbean.

By Cruise Ship

San Juan is the second-largest port in the western hemisphere, and it is a port of call or point of origin for nearly two dozen cruise-ship lines. The cruise-ship docks are at the piers along Calle La Marina in Old San Juan.

Some of the most popular cruise-ship lines serving San Juan include:

- **Carnival Cruise Lines** (866/299-5698, 800/327-9501, www.carnival.com)
- **Celebrity Cruises** (800/647-2251, 800/722-5941, 800/280-3423, www.celebritycruises.com)
- **Holland America Line** (877/724-5425, www.hollandamerica.com)
- **Norwegian Cruise Line** (800/327-7030, www.ncl.com)
- **Princess Cruises** (800/PRINCESS— 800/774-6237, 800/421-0522, www.princess.com)
- **Radisson Seven Seas Cruises** (877/505-5370, 800/285-1835, www.rssc.com)
- **Royal Caribbean International** (866/562-7625, 800/327-6700, 305/539-6000, www.royalcaribbean.com)

SAN JUAN

GETTING AROUND

Taxi

Taxis are a terrific way to get around San Juan because you can catch them just about anywhere. In Old San Juan, there are taxi stands at Plaza de Colón, Plaza de Armas, and the Sheraton near the cruise-ship piers. In Condado, you can flag them down on Avenida Ashford or at the Marriott hotel. In Isla Verde, flag one down on Avenida Isla Verde or find them congregating at the Hotel InterContinental. In outlying areas such as Santurce, Bayamón, Hato Rey, or Río Piedras, you can sometimes flag one down on the major thoroughfares, but you might be better off calling one.

There are a number of licensed taxi services that are well regulated. Operators include **Metro Taxi** (787/725-2870), **Major Taxi** (787/723-2460), **Rochdale Radio Taxi** (787/721-1900), and **Capetillo Taxi** (787/758-7000).

Fares between the airport and the piers in Old San Juan are fixed rates. From the airport, the rates are $10 to Isla Verde, $14 to Condado, and $19 to Old San Juan. From the piers, the rates are $12 to Condado and $19 to Isla Verde. Metered fares are $3 minimum, $1.75 initial charge, and $0.10 every 19th of a mile. The first three pieces of luggage are $0.50; additional luggage is $1 a piece. Customers pay all road tolls.

Bus

Autoridad Metropolitana de Autobuses (787/250-6064 or 787/294-0500, ext. 514, www.dtop.gov.pr/ama/mapaindex.htm) is an excellent public bus system that serves the entire metropolitan San Juan area. It's serviced by large air-conditioned vehicles with access for those with disabilities, and the cost is typically a low $0.75 per fare (exact change required). Bus stops are clearly marked along the routes with green signs that say "Parada," except in Old San Juan, where you have to catch the bus at **Covadonga Bus and Trolley Terminal,** the large terminal near the cruise-ship piers at the corner of Calle la Marina and Calle J. A. Corretjer. When waiting for a bus at a Parada,

it is necessary to wave at the driver to get him to stop. Operating hours are Monday–Friday 4:30 A.M.–10 P.M., Saturday–Sunday and holidays 5:30 A.M.–10 P.M.

The most commonly used routes for tourists are B-21 and A-5. Route B-21 starts at the terminal in Old San Juan and travels down Avenida Ashford in Condado and then south along Avenida Muñoz Rivera through Hato Rey to Plaza Las Americas, the island's largest shopping mall. B-21 runs every 20 minutes Monday–Saturday and every 30 minutes on Sunday and holidays.

Route A-5 connects Old San Juan and Isla Verde. The route travels along Avenida Isla Verde, Calle Loíza, Avenida de Diego, and Avenida Ponce de León into Old San Juan. A-5 does not go to Condado. It is possible to get to Condado from this route by transferring to B-21 at Parada 18 by Avenida De Diego, but keep in mind this stop is near a public-housing project in Santurce, which has been the site of violent crime. A-5 runs every seven minutes Monday–Friday, every 15 minutes Saturday, and every 30 minutes Sunday and holidays.

From the airport, visitors can take the C-45 bus to Isla Verde. To get to other parts of the city, it will be necessary to transfer to another route.

There are many other bus routes in San Juan. To obtain a free, detailed map of all routes, visit the bus terminal in Old San Juan. Riders should be aware, though, that buses serve tourist districts as well as housing projects, and some stops are in places where visitors who are unfamiliar with the lay of the land may not want to be. Make sure you know where you are before you disembark.

Trolley

Although Old San Juan is best experienced by foot, a free trolley service runs daily 8 A.M.–10 P.M. throughout the walled town. The south route goes to Plaza de Armas and the piers. The north route goes to both forts and other major sights. You can catch the trolley at the Covadonga Bus and Trolley Terminal by Plaza de Colón, at La Puntilla parking lot on Calle Puntilla, or at marked stops throughout Old San Juan.

Ferry

Agua Expreso (787/729-8714) provides ferry service from Pier 2 in Old San Juan to Cataño across the San Juan Bay daily 6 A.M.–10 P.M. The 10-minute ride costs $0.50 one way. You can also take a commuter car ferry down the Marin Pena Channel south of Santurce, which connects with the Nuevo Centro station of the Tren Urbano.

Train

In 2005, San Juan launched **Tren Urbano** (866/900-1284, www.dtop.gov.pr/ama/rutas/rutas.htm), its first, long-awaited commuter train service. The system runs 10.7 miles, mostly aboveground, and has 16 stations, many of which house a terrific collection of specially commissioned public art. The train connects the communities of Bayamón, the University of Puerto Rico in Río Piedras, Hato Rey, and Santurce at Sagrado Corazón University. The train runs daily 5:30 A.M.–11:30 P.M. Fares are $1.50.

Publico

Publicos are privately owned transport services that operate passenger vans along regular routes from San Juan to areas around the island. This is a very slow but inexpensive way to see the island. Providers include **Blue Line** (787/765-7733) to Río Piedras, Aguadilla, Aguada, Moca, Isabela, and other areas; **Choferes Unidos de Ponce** (787/764-0540) to Ponce and other areas; **Lina Boricua** (787/765-1908) to Lares, Ponce, Jayuya, Utuado, San Sebastián, and other areas; **Linea Caborrojeña** (787/723-9155) to Cabo Rojo, San Germán, and other areas; **Linea Sultana** (787/765-9377) to Mayagüez and other areas; and **Terminal de**

Transportación Pública (787/250-0717) to Fajardo and other areas.

Car

Driving a car in San Juan can be a nerve-rattling experience for drivers not accustomed to inner-city traffic. The sheer volume of cars on the road at any given time can be daunting, and parking on sidewalks or driving up expressway shoulders are not atypical habits of Puerto Rican drivers. But renting a car is one of the best ways to explore the city and its outlying areas. In addition to most major car-rental agencies, there are several local companies that provide comparable services.

Charlie Car Rental (6050 Ave. Isla Verde and 890 Ave. Ashford, 787/728-2418 or 800/289-1227, www.charliecars.com) is a cheap, reliable alternative to the national agencies. Drivers must be at least 21, and those younger than 25 must pay an additional $10 per day surcharge. Free pickup and drop-off at the airport, hotels, and the cruise-ship port is available.

Vias Car Rental (Hotel Villa del Sol, 4 Calle Rosa, Isla Verde, 787/791-4120 or 787/791-2600; Carr. 693, km 8.2, Calle Marginal in Dorado, 787/796-6404 or 787/796-6882; and Carr. 3, km 88.8, Bo. Candelero in Humacao near Palmas del Mar, 787/852-1591 or 787/850-3070; info@viascarrental.com, www.viascarrental.com, daily 8 A.M.–5 P.M.).

Scooter and Motorcycle

San Juan Motorcycle Rentals (102 Verde Mar, Ave. Isla Verde, 787/722-2111 or 787/791-5339) provides an alternative to renting a full-size car with its Vespa-style motor scooters available for rent by the hour. Free pickup and delivery service is provided.

EAST COAST

Puerto Rico's east coast is rich in natural wonders, making it the most popular destination for day-trippers from San Juan. Less than an hour's drive from the island's capital are three quintessential Puerto Rican sights: El Yunque Caribbean National Forest, Balneario La Monserrate (Playa Luquillo), and Bosque Estatal de Piñones, all on the north end of the east coast. Farther east is Fajardo, the island's boating center renowned for its water sports, and Laguna Grande, a bioluminescent lagoon. Fajardo is also the point of departure for the ferry to the islands of Vieques and Culebra.

The southern side of the east coast is less developed and lacks the big-draw tourist sights found farther north, but its sleepy towns and beaches offer a quiet getaway for those wanting to escape the bustle and crowds.

The east coast is also home to several spectacular resorts, including El Conquistador in Fajardo and Palmas del Mar in Humacao, and the whole area is rich in outstanding golf courses.

There are two officially designated scenic drives in the east coast. The **Ruta Flamboyan** (along Carr. 30 from Carr. 52 to Humacao) affords a lovely view of the spectacular *flamboyan* trees that bloom throughout the summer. These huge trees, also known as royal poinciana, have a broad, umbrella-shaped canopy that blooms a brilliant orange-red from June to early August. The **Ruta Coqui** doesn't necessarily get you any closer to its namesake, the *coqui* tree frog, than does a walk through any other forested part of the island. Instead the route (along Carr. 3 from San Juan

HIGHLIGHTS

◖ Bosque Estatal de Piñones: Between the San Juan airport and the town of Loíza, this untouched parcel of natural beauty features several long stretches of wilderness beach, salt flats, mangroves, lagoons, and tropical forest, as well as six miles of bike path and a cluster of food kiosks serving some stellar Puerto Rican fast-food fare (page 56).

◖ El Yunque Caribbean National Forest: Puerto Rico's crowning jewel of natural treasures, the Caribbean National Forest is a 28,000-acre reserve that encompasses a rain forest, hiking trails, observation towers, waterfalls, and natural pools (page 58).

◖ Las Pailas: This natural water slide is formed by a mountain stream cascading over a smooth but rocky descent that bottoms out in a chest-deep pool of crystal-clear water (page 65).

◖ Balneario La Monserrate: Considered by many to be the main island's most beautiful beach, this publicly maintained facility, commonly called Playa Luquillo, features gentle waters, a wide crescent-shaped strip of sand, and a palm grove, which create the picture-perfect idyll of tropical paradise (page 65).

◖ Reserva Natural Las Cabezas de San Juan: Despite its small 300-acre size, the Fajardo nature reserve features seven different ecosystems, including coral reef, turtle grass, sandy beach, rocky beach, lagoon, dry forest, and mangrove forest. Its mangrove-enveloped Laguna Grande is bioluminescent – kayak here on a moonless night to see the water glow green, thanks to the harmless microscopic organisms that live here. It also boasts an 1880 lighthouse (page 68).

LOOK FOR **◖** TO FIND RECOMMENDED SIGHTS, ACTIVITIES, DINING, AND LODGING.

to Humacao) passes by the east coast's most popular attractions—Playa Luquillo and El Yunque—and the town of Fajardo.

PLANNING YOUR TIME

It's actually possible to take a drive-by tour of the east coast's triumvirate of spectacular natural sights—Piñones, El Yunque, and Playa Luquillo—in a single day if you're pressed for time. But a better option is to spend a full day exploring each one. The attractions are less than an hour's drive from San Juan, and only minutes apart from one another.

When it comes to natural treasures, **El Yunque Caribbean National Forest** is Puerto Rico's shining jewel. One of the world's most accessible rain forests, it offers hours of hiking, swimming, and bird-watching in a lush, tropical setting.

Coming in a close second as Puerto Rico's most popular attraction is Playa Luquillo, officially named **Balneario La Monserrate.** This is

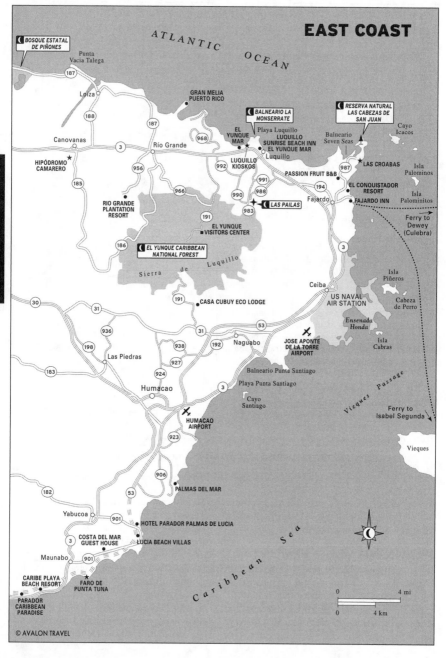

EAST COAST

ATLANTIC OCEAN

BOSQUE ESTATAL DE PIÑONES

Punta Vacia Talega

187

Loíza

188

GRAN MELIA PUERTO RICO

187

Canovanas

968

Río Grande

3

HIPÓDROMO CAMARERO

185

956

966

RIO GRANDE PLANTATION RESORT

186

191

EL YUNQUE VISITORS CENTER

EL YUNQUE CARIBBEAN NATIONAL FOREST

Sierra de Luquillo

BALNEARIO LA MONSERRATE

Playa Luquillo

EL YUNQUE MAR

992

990

988

991

983

LAS PAILAS

LUQUILLO SUNRISE BEACH INN
EL YUNQUE MAR
Luquillo

LUQUILLO KIOSKOS

PASSION FRUIT B&B

194

Fajardo

3

RESERVA NATURAL LAS CABEZAS DE SAN JUAN

Cayo Icacos

Balneario Seven Seas

987

LAS CROABAS

Isla Palominos

EL CONQUISTADOR RESORT
FAJARDO INN

Isla Palominitos

Ferry to Dewey (Culebra)

30

31

31

936

938

927

924

191

192

CASA CUBUY ECO LODGE

53

Naguabo

JOSE APONTE DE LA TORRE AIRPORT

Ceiba

US NAVAL AIR STATION

Ensenada Honda

Isla Piñeros

Cabeza de Perro

Isla Cabras

Vieques Passage

198

Las Piedras

183

Humacao

3

Balneario Punta Santiago
Playa Punta Santiago

Cayo Santiago

HUMACAO AIRPORT

923

Ferry to Isabel Segunda

Vieques

182

906

53

Yabucoa

901

PALMAS DEL MAR

HOTEL PARADOR PALMAS DE LUCIA

COSTA DEL MAR GUEST HOUSE

3

LUCIA BEACH VILLAS

Maunabo

901

CARIBE PLAYA BEACH RESORT

FARO DE PUNTA TUNA

PARADOR CARIBBEAN PARADISE

Caribbean Sea

0   4 mi
0   4 km

© AVALON TRAVEL

what picture postcards are made of: a long crescent of pristine sand gently lapped by the Atlantic Ocean and shaded by a thick palm grove.

Despite its proximity to San Juan, **Bosque Estatal de Piñones** is one of the most beautiful spots of coastal wilderness to be found on the island. It's easy to spend a day hiking or biking through the mangrove forest along the newly constructed bike path, kayaking through its lagoons, and swimming in the Atlantic surf beside palm-lined beaches.

Spending at least a long weekend in Fajardo is recommended for sports enthusiasts who want to enjoy all the boating, diving, fishing, and golfing to be had here. **Reserva Natural Las Cabezas de San Juan** is home to a diversity of ecosystems, as well as **Laguna Grande,** a bioluminescent lagoon that must be experienced at night.

Loíza and Piñones

Loíza holds a special place in Puerto Rican history because it was settled primarily by Yoruba slaves from Nigeria, who were brought over by the Spanish to work the island's sugar and coffee plantations. Emancipated slaves were relocated to Loíza, possibly because the east coast lacked much defense and it was hoped they could help repel foreign intruders. The town also served as a haven for escaped slaves who fled here in increasing numbers. Together they assimilated with the local Taíno Indians.

Loíza is a highly individual, tight-knit community rich in African-Caribbean culture where traditional customs and art forms are preserved and cultivated. Unfortunately, Loíza is also severely economically depressed. There's virtually no industry, and many residents receive some form of public assistance. Not surprisingly, the crime rate is high, with the majority of offenses revolving around the thriving local drug trade.

Loíza's best option for economic viability may be in developing its tourism, because of its proximity to some of the island's most wonderfully unique cultural and natural gems. But that would undoubtedly change the nature of the municipality forever. For now, there's little American influence or tourist industry in Loíza, which makes it the kind of place you should experience sooner rather than later.

Loíza's big claim to fame is its annual weeklong festival, **Fiestas Tradicionales de Santiago Apóstol (St. James Carnival),** a not-to-be-missed celebration for young and old in late July. The festival's complex history, which dates to the Spanish Inquisition, is feted with parades, music, dance, food, and elaborately costumed street theater.

A big part of St. James Carnival is *bomba* and *plena* music, traditional drum-heavy styles of music and dance with African roots that originated in Loíza and thrive there today. Some of *bomba* and *plena's* most celebrated artists are from Loíza.

Among Loíza's greatest charms is its proximity to Piñones, the site of the most gorgeous pristine pieces of natural beauty on the island, **Bosque Estatal de Piñones.** This forest reserve features miles of wild coastline thick with palm groves, mangrove forests and canals, lagoons, sand dunes, and stretches of uninhabited beach as far as the eye can see.

Accommodations are limited to privately owned vacation rentals in Loíza, and dining options are best found in Piñones, which has a dizzying array of terrific roadside food kiosks and several decent restaurants specializing in seafood. It's an ideal day trip from San Juan, 19 miles away.

SIGHTS
Iglesia San Patricio
Iglesia San Patricio (Calle Espíritu Santo, Loíza, 787/876-2229, Mon.–Fri. 8 A.M.–4 P.M.) is claimed to be Puerto Rico's oldest church in continuous use, founded in 1670. It is also known as Espíritu Santo.

BOMBA Y PLENA MUSIC

Bomba y plena refers to two distinctive styles of music that originated with the Nigerian slaves who were captured and shipped to Puerto Rico to work on sugar and coffee plantations.

Bomba is a percussive, call-and-response form of music. The primary instrument is a barril, a drum similar to the conga, originally made by stretching animal skins over discarded wooden barrels. The drums are accompanied with sticks, güiros (a washboard-style percussion instrument made from a gourd) and maracas (one, never two). The call-and-response vocals are secondary in importance to the dance, which is an integral part of bomba. The dancers match each beat of the drums, which goes at a very fast clip, sending the dancers into a frenzy of movement. Performances become a test of endurance between drummers and dancers as they each try to best the other.

Many believe bomba originated in Loíza, while others believe it was brought to Loíza by slaves who were already performing it in West Africa. Nevertheless, Loíza is considered the epicenter of bomba, although Ponce, Mayagüez, Guayama, and Santurce are also important sources of the music.

There are two celebrated families of bomba musicians in Puerto Rico today that reflect two different philosophical approaches to the music. Los Hermanos Ayala, sons of the legendary bomba musician and mask-maker Castor Ayala, are based in Loíza, and their style is strictly traditional, consistently fast-paced, and drum-heavy. Their cousins, the Cepedas, are based in Santurce and make what is called Congrejas bomba, a more contemporary evolution of the form influenced by its more urban roots and other musical styles, such as flamenco.

Plena shares features with bomba, but it adds horns and stringed instruments such as the cuatro (a double-stringed guitar-like instrument) to the mix, and the percussive emphasis is less on the bomba drum and more on the pandereta, a small handheld drum similar to a tambourine but without the cymbals. In plena, dance is secondary to the vocals, which consist of a kind of oral record that usually comments on topical subjects such as scandals, politics, or natural disasters. It is believed to have originated in Ponce, but like bomba, its roots are in Puerto Rico's African culture.

Although plena's popularity has abated through the years, there is a renewed interest in preserving and cultivating the form, and strains of it can be heard in salsa music.

Bosque Estatal de Piñones

There's no other place in Puerto Rico like the spectacular Bosque Estatal de Piñones (along Carr. 187 between San Juan and Loíza, 787/791-7750, office Mon.–Fri. 7 A.M.–3:30 P.M.). Stretching from the eastern tip of Isla Verde, San Juan, to the town of Loíza, this pristine reserve is a natural wonderland of deserted beaches; mangrove, pine, and palm forests; sand dunes; coral reefs; bays; salt flats; and lagoons. An important part of the island ecosystem, Piñones is home to 46 species of birds, including a variety of herons and pelicans.

Boca de Congrejas (just east of the Aeropuerto Internacional Luis Muñoz Marín in San Juan and the Congrejas Yacht Club) is the gateway to Piñones from San Juan. At first glance, it looks like a shantytown of wooden shacks and concrete sheds barely clinging to a rocky point that juts into the sea. But you shouldn't bypass Boca de Congrejas. It contains some of the best and cheapest local food you'll find, from stuffed fritters to all varieties of seafood. Walk from kiosk to kiosk and try a little bit of everything. Many items cost only $1. Expect crowds and a party atmosphere on weekends and holidays. Just east of Boca de Congrejas along Carretera 187 are also several bars and nightclubs that keep the place hopping, day and night. Some people caution against venturing here at night, but it can be a fun, adventurous immersion into the local scene if you keep your wits about you. And definitely stop here during the day to stock up on provisions before entering the forest.

Carretera 187 is a narrow two-lane road that winds through Piñones to Loíza from San Juan. Tucked between the thick clusters of palms along the coastal side of the road are unmarked sandy turn-ins that lead to the beach where you can park and walk down the dunes into the water to swim. You'll start to encounter the best swimming beaches around km 9, where the reef recedes from the beach. Another option for a good swimming spot is **Vacia Talega,** a small unmarked crescent beach visible from the road on Carretera 187 just before you cross the river into Loíza. It has a small sandy parking lot but no facilities. This is also a good fishing spot. Piñones is also a popular place for surfing, especially at **Aviones,** just past Boca de Congrejas.

In addition to swimming, surfing, and fishing, a major draw for Piñones is the **Paseo Piñones Bike Path,** a six-mile-long system of paved trails and boardwalks, which provides an excellent way to explore the forest. Bikes are available for rent at the restaurant **El Pulpo Loco** (Carr. 187, km 4.5, 787/791-8382, 10 A.M.–6 P.M.) for about $25 a day.

Venture away from the coast into the forest's interior and you encounter two lagoons, **Laguna de Piñones** and **Laguna la Torrecilla.** The best way to explore these rich mangrove ecosystems is by kayak. To reach the launch site, turn inland off Carretera 187 at km 9 and follow the sign pointing to the Bosque Estatal de Piñones office. A couple of tour operators in the area offer kayak tours of the lagoons and hiking tours of the forest.

It is possible to take a bus (B-40 or B-45) from Isla Verde to Boca de Congrejas or catch a taxi, but the best option for exploring Piñones is to drive there. Just be sure to lock your car, keep it in sight as much as possible, and don't leave anything of value visible inside.

SPORTS AND RECREATION
Piñones Ecotours (Carr. 187 at Boca de Congrejas Bridge, 787/272-0005, fax 787/789-1730, ecotours@caribe.net) offers biking, hiking, and kayak tours in Bosque Estatal de Piñones. Gear rental is also available.

ENTERTAINMENT AND EVENTS
Fiestas Tradicionales de Santiago Apóstol (St. James Carnival) is one of Puerto Rico's liveliest and most colorful festivals, spanning about six days around July 25. Based in Plaza de Recreo de Loíza, the festival features lots of costumed parades, dances, street pageants, concerts, and traditional food vendors. Ostensibly a celebration of the town's patron saint, St. Patrick, religion takes a back seat to this raucous street party that has origins in 13th-century Spain but is heavily influenced by African traditions. At the center of the celebration is a street pageant in which costumed caballeros (Spanish knights), masked *vejigantes* (Moors), and *locas* (trickster men dressed as old women) reenact Spain's defeat of the Moors. The colorful *vejigante* mask, made from coconut shell, wire, and papier-mâché and featuring protruding horns, has become a highly collectible, iconic symbol of the festival and Puerto Rico as a whole, and there are several local artisans in the area who produce them. St. James Carnival is also a prime place to revel in the African-influenced *bomba* music, which is performed late into the night.

SHOPPING
Estudio de Arte Samuel Lind (Carr. 187, km 6.6, Loíza, 787/876-1494, fax 787/876-1499, loizano@prtc.net, www.studioporto.com/guestsamuellind, Wed.–Sun. 10 A.M.–5 P.M.) is open to the public for the sale of paintings, prints, and sculptures by artist Samuel Lind.

Artesanías Castor Ayala (Carr. 187, km 6.6, 787/876-1130, rayala@caribe.net, daily 9 A.M.–6 P.M.) sells highly collectible *vejigante* masks made by second-generation master mask-maker Raul Ayala.

ACCOMMODATIONS
The best option for accommodations in Loíza and Piñones is an **apartment rental** in one of

the many new, modern, gated condominium developments that have cropped up. Several are on the beach. For information, visit www.vacationrentals411.com, www.rentalo.com, and www.vrbo.com.

FOOD

The casual no-frills dining options are endless at Boca de Congrejas in Piñones and a little farther eastward along Carretera 187. In addition to dozens of kiosks selling fritters and *coco frio* (chilled coconut milk served straight from the shell), there are several casual restaurants selling traditional Puerto Rican cuisine, mostly seafood, for a pittance. Options include **Pulpo Loco by the Sea** (Carr. 187, km 4.5, Piñones, 787/791-8382) and **The Reef** (Carr. 187, km 1, Piñones, 787/791-1973).

Soleil Beach Club (Carr. 187, km 4.6, Piñones, 787/253-1033, www.soleilbeachclub.com, Sun.–Thurs. 11 A.M.–11 P.M., Fri.–Sat.

11 A.M.–2 A.M., $10–39) is the closest thing Piñones has to fine dining, but the atmosphere is still appropriately casual, considering its beachfront location. The two-level restaurant serves traditional Puerto Rican cuisine, including pumpkin soup and crab stew, as well as creative Caribbean cuisine like pan-roasted *dorado* and rock lobster. On weekend nights the place turns into a nightclub when salsa bands and DJs provide the entertainment. The restaurant also offers free transportation to and from your hotel.

PRACTICALITIES

The Loíza **tourist office** (787/886-3628 or 787/876-3570, fax 787/256-2570, Mon.–Fri. 8 A.M.–noon and 1–4:30 P.M.) isn't often open, but it's across the street from Iglesia San Patricio on the plaza. **Juan Carlos Transportation** (787/876-3628 or 787/374-1056, daily 8 A.M.–5 P.M.) offers taxi service and tours around Loíza.

Río Grande

The area that comprises Río Grande saw much fighting between Spanish settlers and the Taíno and Carib Indians. Once the Indian populations dwindled, it became an important agricultural area thanks to the many rivers (Herrera, Espíritu Santo, Mameyes, Sonador, Grande, La Mina) that run through it. Many plantations growing sugarcane and coffee were established here.

Today Río Grande is best known as "The City of El Yunque" because 45 percent of the Caribbean National Forest, as well as the popular El Yunque Recreation Area, is here. It's also a popular golf destination.

◀ EL YUNQUE CARIBBEAN NATIONAL FOREST

It is commonly called El Yunque rain forest, but the official name of this spectacular natural preserve is the Caribbean National Forest. The name El Yunque technically refers to the forest's second-highest peak (3,469 feet), and

a waterfall in El Yunque

it's also the name of the forest's recreational area. But regardless of its moniker, it is without a doubt Puerto Rico's crowning jewel of natural treasures.

The only tropical forest in the U.S. National Forest System—not to mention the smallest and most ecologically diverse—the Caribbean National Forest is a must-see for visitors to Puerto Rico. Nearly half of the 28,000-acre area contains some of the only virgin forest remaining on the island, which was completely covered in forest when Columbus arrived in 1493. It also contains one of the world's most accessible rain forests.

El Yunque is about 35 minutes east of San Juan off Carretera 3. Go south on Carretera 191 and it will take you into the forest and to El Portal Tropical Forest Center.

History

The name El Yunque is believed to be a Spanish derivation of the Taíno Indian name for the area, Yuke, which means "white earth" because the mountaintops are often covered in clouds. The Taíno believed that El Yunque was a sacred place and home to their gods, the most powerful and revered being Yuquiyu, who protected mortals from evil. The Taíno visited the forest to cut trees, vines, and palm fronds to make canoes, baskets, and roofing thatch, and to gather its abundance of fruits, roots, and medicinal plants. It is also believed that religious ceremonies and rituals were held here. Many petroglyphs can be found carved into rocks and boulders throughout the forest.

Upon the arrival of Spanish settlers, attempts were made to exploit the forest's resources. The timber industry initiated forestation, and copper mining was pursued. But in 1876, King Alfonso XII of Spain decreed 12,300 acres of the forest a preserve, making it one of the oldest forest reserves in the western hemisphere. In 1903, after the United States gained control of Puerto Rico following the Spanish-American War, President Theodore Roosevelt designated the area the Luquillo Forest Reserve, and it was eventually expanded to its current size. Further securing its safekeeping, the United Nations

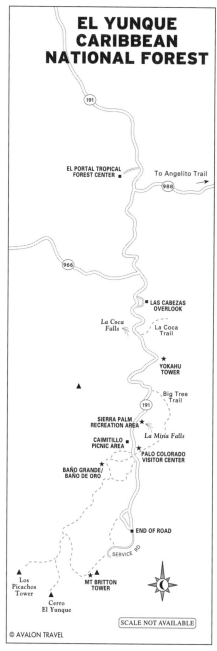

EL YUNQUE CARIBBEAN NATIONAL FOREST

191

EL PORTAL TROPICAL FOREST CENTER ■   To Angelito Trail →

988

966

■ LAS CABEZAS OVERLOOK

La Coca Falls   La Coca Trail

★ YOKAHU TOWER

Big Tree Trail

191

SIERRA PALM RECREATION AREA ★

CAIMITILLO PICNIC AREA ■   La Mina Falls

★ PALO COLORADO VISITOR CENTER

BAÑO GRANDE/ BAÑO DE ORO ★

■ END OF ROAD

SERVICE RD

Los Picachos Tower ▲   ★ ▲ MT BRITTON TOWER

▲ Cerro El Yunque

SCALE NOT AVAILABLE

© AVALON TRAVEL

EAST COAST

designated it as part of the international network of biosphere reserves in 1976.

Flora and Fauna

More than 240 inches of rain—100 billion gallons!—falls annually in the forest, making it a rich habitat for moisture-loving flora and fauna. It is home to more than 1,000 plant species, including 50 types of orchids, 150 ferns, and 240 species of trees, 23 of which are endemic only to El Yunque.

The Caribbean National Forest is in the Sierra de Luquillo, with mountains ranging in height from 600 feet to more than 3,500 feet above sea level, and it contains four distinct forests. Most of the area is covered in the **Tabonuco Forest,** found in areas up to 2,000 feet above sea level. This is the most dramatic part of the forest and site of the true rain forest. The dominant tree species is the *tabonuco,* which grows up to 125 feet in height and is distinguished by its huge dark-green canopy and straight trunk, which has a smooth whitish bark.

The **Sierra Palm Forest** is found along steep slopes and near rivers and creeks more than 1,500 feet above sea level. Its dominant tree, the sierra palm, is easily identified by the thick skirt of exposed roots around its base, which is an adaptation that allows it to thrive in the wet soil. The **Palo Colorado Forest** is found in valleys and slopes at an altitude between 2,000 feet and 3,000 feet. The dominant tree is the *palo colorado,* also known as swamp cyrilla, which is characterized by its thick twisted trunk and red bark. Most of these trees have been around for ages—some reportedly more than 1,000 years.

On the uppermost peaks of El Yunque, between 2,500 and 3,500 feet above sea level, is the **Cloud Forest,** also known as the Dwarf or Elfin Forest. This is a nearly mystical, otherworldly place where constant wind and moisture have stunted and twisted the dense vegetation. Roots snake across the windswept ground in thick tangles, and the trees, which don't exceed 12 feet in height, are covered with moss and algae. Here you also find many species of ferns and bromeliads, which bloom with brilliant red flowers. The air is cool, and visibility is often obscured by misty cloud covering.

Wildlife

The majority of El Yunque's wildlife falls into three categories: birds, reptiles, and amphibians. There are more than 50 species of birds in the forest; the rarest and most beloved is the Puerto Rican parrot, which is classified as endangered. In 1987 an extensive program was initiated to try to bolster the population, though its success has been limited so far. Today there are about 35 Puerto Rican parrots living in the Caribbean National Forest. You're highly unlikely to spot one, but just in case, keep your eyes peeled for a foot-long, bright green Amazon parrot with blue wing tips, white eye rings, and a red band above its beak. When in flight, it emits a repetitive call that sounds like a bugle.

Other species of birds found in El Yunque include the sharp-skinned hawk, the broadwing hawk, the bananaquit, the Puerto Rican tody, the red-legged thrush, the Puerto Rican lizard-cuckoo, the green mango, the Puerto Rican emerald, the Puerto Rican woodpecker, the elfin woods warbler, the Puerto Rican bullfinch, and the stripe-headed tanager.

Even more beloved than the Puerto Rican parrot is the tiny *coqui* tree frog. There are 16 varieties of the species on the island, 13 of which live in El Yunque. You're only slightly more likely to see a *coqui* than a Puerto Rican parrot, but you're sure to hear its distinctive "co-QUI" call, particularly after a rain or at dusk. Even more elusive is the Puerto Rican boa, a nonpoisonous snake that reaches lengths exceeding six feet.

Probably the most likely creature to be spotted in El Yunque is one of its many species of lizards. They are as common as ants at a picnic. The large Puerto Rican giant green lizard, which can grow as big as a cat, is commonly found along the limestone hills, and the smaller *anoli,* of which there are eight species, are ubiquitous.

The only mammals native to Puerto Rico are bats, of which there are 11 species in El Yunque. But rats and mongooses have been introduced to the island and now live in the forest. The rats were inadvertently brought over on trade ships and thrived on the island's sugar plantations. The mongooses were imported in a misguided attempt to control the rat population. They are vicious creatures and carriers of rabies, so give them a wide berth if you encounter them.

Recreation

The main thoroughfare through El Yunque is Carretera 191, which once completely bisected the forest from north to south, but recurrent landslides convinced engineers that the soil was too unstable to sustain a roadway at the forest's highest peaks. The forest is still accessible from the north and south on Carretera 191, but its midsection has been permanently closed. Most visitors to El Yunque drive in from the north end of Carretera 191 because it passes through the El Yunque Recreation Area. But there are efforts under way to close the north end of Carretera 191 and replace car traffic in the forest with a public transportation system to reduce the damaging effects of auto emissions.

The official entrance to the forest is **El Portal Tropical Forest Center** (Carr. 191, km 4, 787/888-1880, daily 9 A.M.–5 P.M., $3 adults, $1.50 children 4–12, free children under 4), a striking piece of architecture designed by the local firm Sierra Cardona Ferrer. Built in 1996, the bright white building is a modern interpretation of the traditional pavilion-style structure seen throughout the island. An elevated walkway leads visitors to its open-air interior filled with interactive educational displays. There are also an excellent gift shop heavy on educational materials, bathroom facilities, and a small screening room that continuously shows a film about the forest alternately in English and Spanish. This is also the place to obtain camping permits and arrange guided tours.

Travel farther south into the forest and you enter **El Yunque Recreation Area,** which encompasses El Yunque peak and the surrounding area, and which contains the forest's major tourist sights. The first stop you encounter is **La Coca Falls** (Carr. 191, km 8.1), the most accessible and photographed waterfall in the forest. It has an 85-foot drop and a constant flow of rushing water. There's plenty of parking space and a small snack bar nearby because this is also the trailhead for La Coca Trail. The next stop on the route is **Yokahu Tower** (Carr. 191, km 8.8), a 69-foot-high observation tower built in 1963 from where you have terrific views of the forest and the Atlantic Ocean. Farther south is **Sierra Palm Recreation Area** (Carr. 191, km 11.3), offering more food concessions, restrooms, and a picnic area. Across the street is the Caimitillo Trailhead. The last stop is **Palo Colorado Visitors Center** (Carr. 191, km 11.8), an information center with still another snack bar and picnic area. Across the street is a short hike to **Baño Grande,** a picturesque stone pool built in the 1930s by the Civilian Conservation Corps. Slightly south of Palo Colorado is another pool, **Baño de Oro,** also built by the CCC. Although visitors are no longer allowed to swim in the pools, they're lovely spots that provide great photo opportunities. Palo Colorado is also the site of La Mina Trailhead and the Baño de Oro Trailhead.

Just before your reach the end of Carretera 191, the road intersects at kilometer 12.6 with a small loop road called Carretera 9938. This road takes you to the trailhead for Mount Britton Trail, which leads to **Mount Britton Tower,** built by the CCC. If visibility is good, you can see the south coast from here. From Mount Britton Trail, you can pick up the Mount Britton Spur Trail to the observation deck on the peak of El Yunque and **Los Picachos Tower,** another CCC tower.

Despite what many visitors might think, there is more to the Caribbean National Forest than El Yunque Recreation Center. In fact, the forest stretches way beyond Río Grande into the municipalities of Ceiba, Canóvanos, Fajardo, Naguabo, Luquillo, and Las Piedras. Many locals actually prefer the southern and western sides of the forest because they're less likely to attract busloads of tourists and they

EAST COAST

feature plenty of waterfalls and natural pools for swimming. To explore the western side, take Carretera 186 south from Carretera 3. To explore the southern side from Naguabo, proceed west on Carretera 31, and go north on Carretera 191.

Trails

Although it's possible to do a quick drive-by tour of El Yunque, the only way to fully appreciate its beauty and majesty is to park the car and hike into the jungle. It doesn't take more than a couple of dozen steps to become completely enveloped by the dense lush foliage. One of the greatest joys of hiking in El Yunque is the sound. Here the aural assault of the 21st century is replaced by a palpable hush and the comforting, sensual, eternal sounds of water—dripping, gurgling, rushing, raining. It's more restorative than a dozen trips to the spa.

There are 12 trails spanning about 14 miles in El Yunque. Many of the trails are paved or covered in gravel because the constant rain and erosive soil would require continuous maintenance to keep them passable. Nonetheless, hiking boots with good tread are a necessity. Even paved trails can be slippery and muddy. The warm air and high humidity also require frequent hydration, so bring plenty of water. And naturally, it rains a lot, so light rain gear is recommended. Avoid streams during heavy rains as flash floods can occur. Primitive camping is permitted in some areas. Permits are required and can be obtained at El Portal Tropical Forest Center.

The following trails are found in El Yunque Recreation Area. All trail lengths and hiking times are approximate.

Angelito Trail (0.5 mile, 15 minutes, easy, clay and gravel) crosses a stream and leads to Las Damas, a natural pool in the Mameyes River. To get to the trailhead, proceed south on Carretera 191 just past El Portal and turn left on Carretera 988, 0.25 mile past Puente Roto Bridge.

La Coca Trail (2 miles, 1 hour, moderate to strenuous, gravel) starts at La Coca Falls and requires navigating over rocks to cross a couple of streams.

La Mina Trail (0.5 mile, 25 minutes, moderate, paved and steps) starts at Palo Colorado and follows the La Mina River, ending at La Mina waterfall, where it connects with Big Tree Trail.

Big Tree Trail (1 mile, 35 minutes, moderate, paved and steps) is an interpretive trail with signs in Spanish and English. It passes through Tabonuco Forest, over streams, and ends at La Mina waterfall, where it connects to La Mina Trail. The trailhead is by a small parking area at Carretera 191, km 10.2.

Caimitillo Trail (0.5 mile, 25 minutes, easy, paved and steps) begins at Sierra Palm Recreation Area and crosses a stream. Along the way are a picnic area and structures used by the Puerto Rican parrot recovery program. It connects to the Palo Colorado Visitors Center and El Yunque Trail.

Baño de Oro Trail (0.25 mile, 20 minutes, moderate, paved and gravel) starts just south of the Palo Colorado Visitors Center and passes by Baño de Oro before connecting with El Yunque Trail.

El Yunque Trail (2.5 miles, 1 hour, strenuous, paved and gravel) is one of the forest's longest and most strenuous hikes. It starts a little north of the Palo Colorado Visitors Center and climbs to an altitude of 3,400 feet. Along the way it passes several rain shelters, through the Cloud Forest, and ends at the peak of El Yunque. The lower part of the trail is accessible from Caimatillo Trail and Baño de Oro Trail. The higher reaches of the trail connect with Mount Britton Trail and Los Picachos Tower Trail.

Mount Britton Trail (1 mile, 45 minutes, strenuous, paved) starts at Carretera 9938, a loop road at the end of Carretera 191. It is an uphill hike through the Tabonuco, Sierra Palm, and Cloud Forests. The trail crosses two streams and runs along a service road for a short distance—if you're not sure which way to go, just keep heading straight up. It ends at the Mount Britton Tower, built in the 1930s by the Civilian Conservation Corps.

Mount Britton Spur (1 mile, 30 minutes, moderate, paved) connects Mount Britton Trail to El Yunque Trail.

Los Picachos Trail (0.25 mile, 25 minutes, strenuous, unpaved and steps) is a steep ascent from El Yunque Trail to an observation deck built by the CCC.

The forest's remaining two trails are outside El Yunque Recreation Center on the western side of the forest. The trails are unpaved, muddy, not maintained, and often overgrown in parts. Long sleeves and pants are recommended for protection against brush, some of which can cause skin irritation on contact. These trails are for adventurous hikers who really want to get away from it all.

Trade Winds Trail (4 miles, 4 hours, strenuous, primitive) is the forest's longest trail. To reach the trailhead, drive all the way through El Yunque Recreation Area to the end of Carretera 191 where the road is closed. Be mindful not to block the gate. Walk past the gate 0.25 mile to the trailhead. The trail ascends to the peak of El Toro, the highest peak in the forest, where it connects with the El Toro Trail.

El Toro Trail (2 miles, 3 hours, difficult, primitive) starts at Carretera 186, km 10.6, and traverses Tabonuco, Sierra Palm, and Cloud forests. It connects with the Trade Winds Trail.

SPORTS AND RECREATION
Golf
What made Río Grande a fertile, well-hydrated place for growing sugarcane and coffee has made it an excellent place for golf courses today. A new course designed by Robert Trent Jones Jr. is slated to open in 2010 at the St. Regis Resort, currently under development at Bahía Beach Plantation.

Río Mar Beach Resort (Carr. 968, km 1.4, 787/888-8811, www.wyndhamriomar .com, 6:30 A.M.–6:30 P.M., greens fees $150–175 for resort guests, $185–200 nonguests, call 24 hours in advance) has two courses. Ocean Course, built in 1975 by George and Tom Fazio, offers excellent views of the Atlantic Ocean and one of the best-rated holes (No. 16) on the island. River Course, an 18-hole grass course with water in play built in 1997 by Greg Norman, runs along the Río Mameyes. There's

also a 35,000-square-foot clubhouse. Golf club rentals are available.

Trump International Golf Club (100 Club House Dr., Rio Grande, 787/657-2000, www .trumpgolfclubpuertorico.com, daily dawn–dusk), formerly the Coco Beach Golf and Country Club, offers 36 holes of ocean-side golf on courses designed by Tom Kite and Bruce Besse. Food and beverage service is provided on the course and in the clubhouse, which also has a pro shop. There is a putting green and driving range as well. In 2008 it hosted the PGA Tour's Puerto Rico Open.

Hiking
AdvenTours (787/889-0251, www.adventours pr.com) is an ecotourism operator offering expeditions throughout the island, including night hikes and bike tours of El Yunque. Expeditions depart from La Castia in Old San Juan. Reservations are required.

ENTERTAINMENT
Casinos
There are two casinos in Río Grande. **Gran Melia Puerto Rico** (1000 Coco Beach Blvd., Carr. 3 at Carr. 955, 787/809-1770, www .gran-melia-puerto-rico.com, 5 P.M.–2 A.M.) has a small casino with 130 slot machines, blackjack, progressive blackjack, roulette, craps, poker, and Texas hold 'em. **Río Mar Beach Resort** (Carr. 968, km 1.4, 787/888-6000, www.wyndhamriomar.com, Sun.–Thurs. 10 P.M.–2 A.M., Fri.–Sat. 10 A.M.–4 A.M.) is even smaller space-wise, but it has 190 slots, blackjack, roulette, craps, Caribbean poker, Texas hold 'em, and three-card poker.

Horse Racing
Hipódromo Camarero (Carr. 3, km 15.3, Canóvanas, 787/876-2450, www.hipodromo camarero.com, Mon., Wed., and Fri.–Sun.; first race begins 2:45 P.M. except Sun., when it begins at 2:15 P.M.; last race 6 P.M.; admission free) is technically in the municipality of Canóvanas, just east of Río Grande. Watch the races with food and beverage service from the grandstand, the clubhouse, or the Terrace Room restaurant.

You can also watch the action on live monitors in the Winners Sports Bar.

SHOPPING

Coqui International (54 Calle Principal, Palmer, off Carr. 191 on the way to El Yunque, 787/887-0770, www.coquistores.com, Mon.–Sat. 10 A.M.–6 P.M., Sun. noon–6 P.M.) is a huge gallery selling a wide selection of crafts by local artisans as well as artisans from Haiti and the Dominican Republic. It's a great place to buy contemporary and traditional *vejigante* masks, plus paintings, hammocks, food items, candles, and jewelry. Technically it is located in the community of Palmer, but it's on the way to the El Yunque rain forest. If you're traveling east on Carretera 3 from San Juan, turn right on Carretera 191 then left on Calle Principal; the store is on the left.

ACCOMMODATIONS

Río Grande Plantation Eco Resort (Carr. 956, km 4.2, Guzmán Abajo, 787/887-2779 or 787/887-5822, fax 787/888-3239, info@ riograndeplantation.com, www.riogrande plantation.com, $136 s, $163–272 one-room villa, $272 two-room villa, plus 9 percent tax) is a unique, rustic property at the base of the Caribbean National Forest. It features 22 accommodations that run the gamut from single rooms to two-level villas with balconies overlooking the Río Grande. The buildings are a tad shabby and the furnishings a bit worn, but most rooms are large and comfortable and feature modern bathrooms, satellite TV, VCRs, air-conditioning, and kitchenettes. Amenities include a swimming pool, a basketball court, a game room, a business office, and several large event pavilions. What really makes this property interesting is its massive grounds, which have been left in their natural wooded state and feature several hiking trails. Las Tasqueria serves a modest menu daily 11 A.M.–11 P.M. This is a popular family vacation spot for Puerto Rican families.

Gran Melia Puerto Rico (1000 Coco Beach Blvd., Carr. 3 at Carr. 955, 787/809-1770 or 866/436-3542, fax 787/807-1785, www .gran-melia-puerto-rico.com, $169–350 s/d, plus taxes and resort fees) is a large 500-unit luxury resort, formerly known as Paradisus Puerto Rico. All accommodations are suites or villas and come with balconies or terraces, marble baths, air-conditioning, hair dryers, room safes, minibars, satellite TV, high-speed Internet, and room service. It has three restaurants serving Puerto Rican, Asian, and Italian fare, as well as two bars. Amenities include a lovely lagoon-style swimming pool, a spa and health club, three lighted tennis courts, and access to Trump International Golf Clubs. Guests can upgrade to what's called Royal Service to receive butler service and access to a private lounge and adults-only pool.

FOOD

Most of the notable dining options in Río Grande are limited to the restaurants at the Gran Melia Puerto Rico and Río Mar resorts. But there is one local nonhotel option worth checking out: **Antojitos Puertorriqueños** (No. 60, Carr. 968, Barrio Las Coles, 787/888-7378, daily 10 A.M.–9 P.M.) serves excellent local cuisine, including stuffed *mofongo* and *tostones,* rice and crab, *chillo* in garlic sauce, and salmon. Check out the changing exhibits of work by local artists.

And if you want to try some excellent Caribbean-style sangria, pay a visit to **Los Paraos Liquors** (54 Calle Pimentel, off Carr. 3, Río Grande, 787/888-3320, daily noon–2 A.M.), a modest-looking roadside liquor store with a popular outdoor stand-up bar. Those in the know flock here to buy the outstanding homemade sangria, a delicious pale-pink concoction packed with fresh fruit juices and sold in recycled liquor bottles for $7.50 apiece. Stock up! Once you try it, you'll want more. If traveling east on Carretera 3, turn left by the giant parrot sculptures onto Carretera 187R, and then take an immediate left on the one-way street. It's on the right—look for the large sign above the awning.

Luquillo

Luquillo is renowned for its breathtakingly beautiful public beach, most commonly referred to as Playa Luquillo, although its proper name is Balneario La Monserrate. Many consider this the finest beach on the main island, and its proximity to San Juan makes it one of the most popular among visitors.

Unfortunately, Luquillo's town center has undergone a recent renovation that has transformed its uncommonly large plaza into a modernist concrete pad with nary a tree in sight. There's little reason to tarry here, except to stop by Victor's Place for a stellar seafood meal. Instead, head over to the coastal side of town, where you'll find great swimming, surfing, and the island's popular array of kiosks selling fabulous fried fare for a pittance.

◖ LAS PAILAS

Las Pailas (Carr. 983, Barrio Yuquiyu, Luquillo) is about as off the beaten path as you can get. This natural waterslide is formed by a mountain stream cascading over a smooth but rocky descent that bottoms out in a chest-deep pool of crystal-clear water. Locals come here on weekends to mount the "horse," a saddle-shaped rock at the top of the descent, and slide down the rocks, landing in the natural pool below. If you're lucky, you'll see expert showboaters slide down on their bellies, face first, or even on foot. This is not an official tourist site. There are no signs, facilities, parking, or rules, although visitors should be mindful of respecting the property and not leave any trash behind. Although it's primarily a locals' spot, visitors are welcome, especially if they prove their mettle by taking a ride. To get here from San Juan, take Highway 3 east. Turn right on Carretera 992 and go toward Sabana, and then turn right on Carretera 983. Las Pailas is behind the homes that line the right side of the road. The best access is behind house No. 6051, distinguished by a cyclone fence. Homeowners along this stretch allow visitors to park for $5 and will point you toward a well-worn path

that takes you to the nearby shoals. If you get lost, just ask.

BEACHES
◖ Balneario La Monserrate

Balneario La Monserrate, or Playa Luquillo (Carr. 3, east of San Juan, 787/889-5871, daily 8:30 A.M.–5:30 P.M.), is the kind of place people dream of when they envision an island paradise. A thick grove of tall, shady coconut palm trees sways in the breeze over a mile-long wide crescent of pristine sand gently lapped by the Atlantic Ocean. The only signs of civilization are a clean modern complex of bathrooms and showers, some covered picnic shelters, and a couple of snack bars serving fritters and piña coladas. Camping is permitted in a grassy area with picnic tables and grills on the western side. Rates are $13, $17 with electricity. Call 787/889-5871 for reservations.

The only drawback to this idyllic spot is

© SUZANNE VAN ATTEN

taking a ride down Las Pailas in Luquillo

that it gets packed with beachgoers on weekends, holidays, and during the summer, when beach chairs and umbrellas are available for rent and lifeguards keep an eye on things. If you want solitude, visit on a weekday during the low season, and you'll practically have the place to yourself.

On the far eastern side of the beach is **Mar Sin Barreras** (Sea Without Barriers), a staffed, wheelchair-accessible beach that caters to visitors with disabilities. In addition to a system of ramps that permits those in wheelchairs to roll right into the water, there are accessible bathrooms, showers, parking, and picnic shelters. The facility also rents special wheelchairs for entering the water.

Other Beaches

Although Balneario La Monserrate gets all the accolades and attention, it isn't the only beach in Luquillo. A newly designated nature preserve, **La Selva Natural Reserve** (Carr. 193, just east of Luquillo) is a 3,240-acre tract of land comprised of wetlands, mangroves, coastal forest, and pristine beaches ideal for swimming and surfing—just beware of the reefs. This is an important nesting site for leatherback turtles.

In the town of Luquillo along Carretera 193 is **Playa Azul,** a sandy crescent beach great for swimming and snorkeling. Parking is limited, and there are no facilities besides a few street vendors selling snacks. Farther eastward on Calle Herminio Diaz Navarro is **La Pared,** a great surfing spot adjacent to a picturesque seawall just one block from Luquillo's central plaza.

SPORTS AND RECREATION

La Selva Surf Shop (250 Fernandez Garcia, one block south of the plaza, 787/889-6205, daily 9 A.M.–5 P.M.) is a great source for tips on surfing in the area. In addition to selling a variety of beach and surfing accessories, it rents surfboards ($30 per day) and boogie boards ($10 per day).

Hacienda Carabalí (Carr. 992, km 3, 787/889-5820 or 787/889-4954, www

.haciendacarabalipuertorico.com) is a 600-acre ranch offering guided horseback-riding tours on Paso Finos along mountainside and beachfront trails, along with ATV tours, mountain biking, and go-karts.

ACCOMMODATIONS

Despite Luquillo's popularity as a tourist destination for locals and international travelers alike, it has a dearth of overnight accommodations.

Luquillo Sunrise Beach Inn (A3 Ocean Blvd., 787/409-2929, info@luquillosunrise. com, www.luquillosunrise.com, $115–135 s/d, $210 suite, $195 two-bedroom casita, plus 9 percent tax) is a spiffy new 15-unit property right across the street from La Pared beach at Calle Herminio Diaz Navarro. Rooms are neat, modern, and comfortable. A restaurant on-site serves breakfast only.

El Yunque Mar (6 Calle 1, 787/889-5555, hotel@yunquemar.com, www.yunquemar.com, $95–110 s/d, suites $225–250, plus 9 percent tax) is a small hotel in a residential area right on Playa Fortuna. This modest, faux Spanish-style hacienda offers 15 clean modern units with air-conditioning and cable TV. Suites come with mini-refrigerators and microwaves. There's no restaurant or bar, but there is a small pool.

FOOD

◖ **Luquillo Kioskos** (Carr. 3) is nearly as popular an attraction in Luquillo as Balneario La Monserrate. Along Carretera 3 just before you approach Luquillo from San Juan, this long stretch of 80-plus side-by-side shacks is one of the best places to experience Puerto Rico's array of traditional fritters. Shaped like discs, half moons, cigars, boats, and balls, these crispy deep-fried goodies come stuffed with a varied combination of meat, crab, cheese, plantain, coconut, and more. Each kiosk serves nearly identical fare at stand-up bars where you can eat on your feet or seated at a table nearby. Pick one of each (they're only $1–3 apiece) and wash it all down with a cold beer, a cocktail, or *coco frio,* ice-cold coconut juice served from the shell. Be sure to buy a bag of *coco dulce,*

KIOSK CUISINE

© SUZANNE VAN ATTEN

one of many food kiosks in Luquillo

The roadways all over Puerto Rico are dotted with countless lean-tos, shacks, pavilions, tents, and trucks where enterprising cooks sell a variety of mostly fried local delicacies. For the uninitiated, the assortment of fried blobs, discs, and turnovers can be daunting. But if you want a truly traditional Puerto Rican experience, muster your courage, pop an antacid, and dive into an adventurous array of some of the freshest, tastiest dining on the island.

Most items sell for as little as a dollar apiece, are served not on plates but wrapped in napkins, and are eaten standing up. A variety of hot sauces is usually on hand to spice things up if desired, and nothing washes it all down better than an ice-cold Medalla beer.

Some of the most common items served include:

- **Alcapurria:** Grated, mashed plantain and/or *yautia* (taro root) stuffed with crab or beef and deep-fried. They look like small fried sweet potatoes, fat in the middle, tapered on the ends.

- **Arepa coco:** South American in origin, it's made from mashed or grated coconut mixed with corn flour, formed into a small round patty, and fried. It looks like a small fried disc.

- **Bacalaito:** Mashed codfish mixed into a flour batter and deep-fried. Looks like a big, irregularly shaped funnel cake or "elephant ear" like the kind sold at amusement parks.

- **Barcazas:** Whole plantains sliced length-wise, stuffed with ground beef, topped with cheese. They look like banana boats.

- **Coco dulce:** An immensely sweet confection of fresh, coarsely grated coconut and caramelized sugar. Looks like a brown craggy praline.

- **Coco frio:** Chilled coconuts still in their green husks. A hole is cut in the top and a straw stuck through it. Inside is a refreshing thin coconut milk. After you drink all the liquid, ask your server to chop it in half and scoop the coconut out with a spoon if it's unripe and soft, or you can chunk it out with a knife if it's ripe and hard.

- **Empanada:** Savory circle of pastry stuffed with meat, crab, lobster, shrimp, or fish, folded into a half moon, thickly crimped along the rounded side, and deep-fried. Looks like a giant apple turnover.

- **Papas rellenas:** A big lump of mashed potatoes stuffed with meat and deep-fried. Looks like a fried baseball.

- **Pastele:** Traditionally eaten around the Christmas holidays, the *pastele* is a Puerto Rican version of a tamale featuring mashed plantain, green banana, yucca root, and pork or chicken, wrapped in a banana leaf and steamed. Don't eat the leaf!

- **Pastilillo:** Smaller version of the empanada with a thinner, airier crust. Looks like a small apple turnover.

- **Pinchos:** Chunks of chicken, pork, or fish threaded on a skewer and grilled. Looks like a shish kebab.

- **Pionono:** A thin, lengthwise slice of plantain lightly fried and then wrapped around a patty of meat and egg and deep-fried. Looks like a giant deep-fried crab cake.

- **Taquitos:** Chicken, ground beef, crab, or fish rolled up in a piece of dough and deep-fried. They look like big fat cigars and are sometimes called tacos, but they're nothing like the Mexican version.

sinfully rich patties of sugary coconut, for later. This place can get packed on the weekends and holidays, and the atmosphere can get rowdy at night. Despite the area's rustic nature, most kiosks accept credit and debit cards.

Cafeteria La Exquisita (corner of Calle L. Calzada and Ave. 14 de Julio, on the plaza, 787/633-5551 or 787/370-3537, daily 10 A.M.–2 P.M., $5–8) serves traditional Puerto Rican cuisine, including *arroz con pollo,* rice and beans, pork, *tostones,* and more.

⟨ Erik's Gyros and Deli (352 Calle Fernandez Garcia, at the intersection of Carr. 992 and Carr. 193 right by Carr. 3, 787/889-0615, Mon.–Sat. 7 A.M.–5 P.M., $4–10) is an excellent place to get a cheap Greek-, American-, or Puerto Rican–style breakfast or lunch. This little corner deli serves gyros, burgers, lamb barbecue, Cuban sandwiches, tortilla-style omelets, French toast, and more. It also sells chorizo and serrano ham by the pound.

Fajardo

Fajardo is a bustling little seaside town notable for its many marinas and plethora of sports and recreation opportunities. It's also an excellent seaborne transportation hub to Caribbean points east, where you can catch a ferry or sailboat to Vieques, Culebra, St. Thomas, and beyond.

Although it has a town proper with the requisite plaza and church, the heart of Fajardo can be found along the coast, where hundreds of vessels dock and dozens of seafood restaurants vie to serve fresh fish and Puerto Rican fare to the day-trippers and sports enthusiasts who flock here for the superb diving, fishing, sailing, and golf.

Fajardo is also home to one of the island's bioluminescent lagoons, Laguna Grande, in Reserva Natural Las Cabezas de San Juan. Here you can kayak at night and marvel at the phosphorescent microorganisms that light up the water with a sparkling green glow.

SIGHTS
Balneario Seven Seas

Balneario Seven Seas (Carr. 987, beside Las Cabezas de San Juan, Las Croabas, 787/796-1052, daily 6 A.M.–6 P.M., $3) is a great beach for swimming and snorkeling. For underwater action, check out the reef on the far eastern end of the beach. Camping for RVs and tents is also available, although quarters are close so don't expect much privacy. Call 787/863-8180 for reservations.

Parque Las Croabas

Parque Las Croabas (Carr. 987) is a pleasant waterside park overlooking Bahía Las Croabas, dotted with moored fishing boats. From here you can see the island of Vieques. There are several concrete picnic shelters, poorly maintained bathroom facilities, and a small boat launch. Across the street are several bars and restaurants serving seafood.

Reserva Natural La Cordillera

Reserva Natural La Cordillera, comprised of Icacos, Diablo, Palomino, and Palominitos, is a protected string of small sandy islands just north and east of Fajardo with lots of great snorkeling and diving spots around them. Bring plenty of water and sunscreen—there are no facilities or stores on the islands. To get there, go to the dock in Las Croabas and arrange a ride with one of the boat operators there. They'll drop you off and return later to pick you up. The cost is typically $10 each way. The islands can get crowded on weekends and holidays.

⟨ Reserva Natural Las Cabezas de San Juan

Reserva Natural Las Cabezas de San Juan/ El Faro (Carr. 987, km 6, 787/722-5882, guided tours Wed.–Sun. 9:30 A.M., 10 A.M., 10:30 A.M., 2 P.M., $7 adults, $2 children 11 and younger) is a unique and treasured piece of island property that has been protected from encroaching development. This 316-acre piece of land contains examples of all the island's natural habitats except for the rain forest: coral reefs, turtle grass, sandy and rocky beaches, lagoons, a dry forest, and a mangrove forest. It is home to many endangered wildlife species, including the osprey and the sea turtle, and artifacts of the Igneri Indians, precursors to the Taínos, have been excavated here.

Two main points of interest are found at Las Cabezas de San Juan. One is the neoclassical lighthouse *(el faro),* built by the Spanish in 1880, making it the island's second-oldest lighthouse. Today it houses facilities for scientific research in the areas of ecology, marine biology, geology, and archaeology.

The other highlight of Las Cabezas de San Juan is **Laguna Grande,** a mangrove lagoon filled with microscopic bioluminescent organisms that glow green at night when they sense motion. Several outfitters in the area offer canoe or kayak rides into the lagoon after dark on moonless nights so visitors can witness the biological phenomenon. Swimming in the lagoon is no longer permitted.

This rich nature reserve also features a nature center, hiking trails, a boardwalk, and an observation tower from which you can see El Yunque and nearby islands as far away as Tortola.

Entrance into Las Cabezas de San Juan is by guided tour only. Call for reservations. To get here, take Carretera 3 to the Conquistador Avenue exit and turn left on Carretera 987. The reserve is on the left after Balneario Seven Seas recreation area.

SPORTS AND RECREATION
Snorkeling, Diving, and Sailing

Most water-sports outfitters offer a variety of snorkeling, diving, and sailing opportunities to the northeast coast's natural attractions, as well as to Vieques and Culebra.

Sea Ventures Dive Center (Carr. 3, km 51.2, Fajardo, www.divefajardo.com; and Palmas del Mar Resort, Humacao, www.palmasdel mar.com, 787/863-3483 or 800/739-3483,

fax 787/863-0199) operates three dive centers on the east coast, one in Fajardo, one in Guanica, and the other at Palmas del Mar, offering dive and snorkel trips to local reefs, Vieques, Culebra, and Cayo Santiago (Monkey Island) in Naguabo. Rent equipment or bring your own. The company also operates a dive center at the Copamarina Beach Resort in Guanica. Reservations are required.

Las Tortugas Adventures (4 Calle La Puntilla, San Juan, 787/725-5169, info@kay-ak-pr.com, www.kayak-pr.com) offers a variety of half- and full-day snorkeling and kayak tours on the east coast, launching from Bahía Las Croabas in Fajardo. Tours include Las Cabezas de San Juan in Fajardo, the bioluminescent lagoon, the mangrove forest in Piñones, and excursions to Cayo Icacos, Cayo Diablo, and Monkey Island. No experience is necessary, and all equipment is provided. Reservations are required.

East Island Excursions (Puerto Del Rey Marina, Fajardo, 787/860-3434 or 877/937-4386, fax 787/860-1656, www.eastwindcats .com) offers sailing and snorkeling trips aboard a 62-foot sailing catamaran with a glass bottom and a slide, a 65-foot power catamaran, or a 45-foot catamaran. Excursions are available to Vieques, Culebra, Culebrita, and St. Thomas. Reservations are required.

Caribbean School of Aquatics (Villa Marina, Fajardo, 787/728-6606, www.sail diveparty.com) advertises itself with the slogan "Sail Dive Party" despite the scholarly name of its operation. It offers snorkeling, diving, and sailing trips to Vieques and Culebra aboard catamarans and sailing sloops. Reservations are required.

Traveler (Carr. 987, km 1.3, Villa Marina, Fajardo, 787/863-2821 or 787/396-0995, fax 787/801-0608, puertoricotraveler@hotmail. com, www.travelerpr.com) offers snorkeling and sailing on a 54-foot Catamaran. Trips depart from Villa Marina at 1 P.M., and transportation can be arranged from San Juan. Group rates and charter packages are available.

Kayaking Puerto Rico (787/435-1665 or 787/564-5629, info@kayakingpuertorico.com, www.kayakingpuertorico.com) offers combination kayaking and snorkeling expeditions, as well as bioluminescent plankton tours in Laguna Grande.

Kayaking

Yokahu Kayaks (Carr. 987, km 6.2, Las Croabas, Fajardo, 787/863-5374 or 787/604-7375, yokahukayaks@hotmail.com) offers kayak tours to Laguna Grande in Las Cabezas de San Juan with licensed guides and equipment included. Reservations are required.

Kayaking Puerto Rico (787/435-1665 or 787/564-5629, info@kayakingpuertorico.com, www.kayakingpuertorico.com) offers bioluminescent plankton tours in Laguna Grande, as well as combination kayaking and snorkeling expeditions.

Las Tortugas Adventures (4 Calle La Puntilla, San Juan, 787/725-5169, info@kayak-pr.com, www.kayak-pr.com) offers kayak tours from Bahía Las Croabas to Las Cabezas de San Juan in Fajardo and the mangrove forest in Piñones. No experience is necessary, and all equipment is provided. Reservations are required.

Fishing

Light Tackle Paradise (Marina Puerto Chico, Carr. Road 987, km 2.4, 787/347-4464, $350–450 half-day for 4 or 6 people) offers fishing excursions on 22-foot and 26-foot catamarans or 17-foot skiffs.

Tropical Fishing Charters (787/379-4461 or 787/266-4524, tropicaldeepsea@aol.com, www.tropicalfishingcharters.com) offers year-round big-game fishing, specializing in blue marlin May–October.

Golf and Tennis

Wyndham El Conquistador Resort (1000 Conquistador Ave., 787/863-1000, www.elconresort.com) boasts the Arthur Hills Golf Course (daily 6:30 A.M.–6:30 P.M.), a 72-par hilly course overlooking the Atlantic Ocean and El Yunque rain forest. There are more than 50 bunkers and five water hazards, including a waterfall on the 18th hole. There are

also a driving range and a putting green. It is home to the Ambassador's Cup golf tournament in December. There are also seven tennis courts, four clay and three hard. Four are lit for 24-7 play.

Spa

Golden Door Spa (Wyndham El Conquistador Resort, 1000 Conquistador Ave., 787/863-1000, www.elconresort.com) offers a wide variety of massages, hydrotherapy treatments, facials, reflexology, and energy-balancing treatments, including Reiki and craniosacral.

ENTERTAINMENT AND EVENTS

Carnaval de Fajardo (787/863-1400) is held in early August on Plaza de Recreo, featuring an artisans fair, a carnival, music, food, and arts and crafts.

The Casino at El Conquistador (Wyndham El Conquistador Resort, 1000 Conquistador Ave., 787/863-1000, www.elconresort.com) features two Caribbean stud poker tables, five roulette wheels, three craps tables, 12 blackjack tables, and 224 slot machines.

ACCOMMODATIONS
$50-100

Anchor's Inn (Carr. 987, km 2.7, 787/863-7200, Frenchman@libertypr.net, $62 s, $73 d, $97 t, includes tax) is a good option if you just need a cheap place to crash. The inn is tacked on behind the Anchor's Inn restaurant and is in a parking lot near a fairly busy intersection. Amenities and aesthetics are nil.

$100-150

◀ **The Fajardo Inn** (52 Parcelas Beltrán, 787/860-6000, fax 787/860-5063, info@fajardoinn.com, www.fajardoinn.com, $110–120 s, $132 d, $160 t, $132 junior suite, $175–300 luxury suite, plus 9 percent tax) is a large, bright white complex with 97 units high on a hill, affording gorgeous views of the ocean from one side and the mountains from the other. Formerly a property belonging to the U.S. military, this hotel has undergone a complete overhaul, making it a very pleasant family-friendly place to stay. The rooms are modern, well-maintained, and simply furnished. They all have air-conditioning, cable TV, and telephones, and some have kitchenettes, balconies, mini-refrigerators, and whirlpool baths. On the property are two pools, a playground, miniature golf, laundry facilities, and two restaurants.

Passion Fruit Bed & Breakfast (Carr. 987, Las Croabas, 787/801-0106, gladys@ passionfruitbb.com, www.passionfruitbb .com, $93–114 d, $136 suite, $141 quad, plus taxes, includes full breakfast) offers comfortable, modern accommodations in a brightly colored, three-story structure that houses 11 units named after famous Puerto Ricans. Amenities include air-conditioning, satellite TV, and a pool. Wi-Fi is available in common areas.

Over $250

◀ **El Conquistador Resort and Golden Door Spa** (1000 Conquistador Ave., 787/863-1000, www.elconresort.com, $319–494 s/d), now a Luxury Resorts & Hotels property, is one of Puerto Rico's best-known and most highly regarded luxury resorts. A behemoth property perched atop a dramatic cliff with a stunning panoramic view of the ocean, El Conquistador is more like a small town than a hotel. It boasts 750 rooms in five separate white stucco and terra-cotta complexes set amid beautifully landscaped cobblestone streets, plazas, and fountains. There are a whopping 23 restaurants and bars on-site, as well as a casino, fitness center, full-service spa, seven swimming pools, an ocean-side water park, seven tennis courts, an 18-hole golf course, and a 35-slip marina. Every room has air-conditioning, satellite TV, telephone, minibar, marble bathroom, CD player, VCR, computer and fax connections, coffeemaker, and a sitting area. Snorkeling, scuba diving, and fishing tours and equipment are available on-site. There's also transportation available to the more secluded beaches on nearby Palomino Island.

FOOD
Puerto Rican and Seafood

◀ **La Estacion** (Carr. 987, km 3.5, next to Hotel Conquistador, Las Croabas, Fajardo, 787/863-4481, www.laestacionpr.com, Wed.– Sun. 5 P.M.–midnight, $9–22), owned and operated by Kevin Roth from Brooklyn, New York, and Idalia Garcia from Puerto Rico, is a super-casual oasis of convivial fun and outstanding, freshly prepared cuisine. The kitchen is located in a converted gas station, but the sprawling dining areas are on open air patios appointed with awnings, padded lawn furniture, butterfly chairs, and tabletops surrounded by tiki torches and festive strings of lights. There's also a partially enclosed bar with a juke box filled with contemporary Latino rock and reggaetón tunes and a pool table. The vibe is akin to hanging out in your coolest friend's basement. But it's the food that really puts this place on the map. Everything is charcoal grilled, right outside where you can watch the action—fresh fish of the day, shrimp, *churrasco,* strip steaks, chicken, and burgers. The green papaya salad makes for a refreshing starter. And many of the ingredients are locally sourced. Be sure to order the house cocktail, called the Low Tide. It features rum, Triple Sec, and fresh pineapple and tamarind juices.

Rosa's Sea Food (536 Calle Tablado, Marina Puerto Real, 787/863-0213, Thurs.– Tues. 11 A.M.–10 P.M., $12–30) is a highly recommended spot for traditional Puerto Rican cuisine, especially the grilled fish and lobster.

Restaurante Ocean View (Carr. 987, km 6.8, 787/863-6104, Thurs.–Mon. 11 A.M.–midnight, $10–40) is right across the street from Parque Los Croabas and is a festive casual place to dine on fresh seafood under an open-air pavilion. It serves excellent combination seafood platters, *mofongo,* and paella, and it has a full bar.

Anchor's Inn (Carr. 987, km 2.7, 787/863-7200, Sun.–Mon. and Wed.–Thurs. noon–10 P.M., Fri.–Sat. noon–11 P.M., $8–30) is a whimsical black, white, and red wooden structure that looks something like an old

English seaside inn. The menu primarily comprises steak and seafood, its specialties being paella, stuffed seafood *mofongo*, and *chillo tropical*, featuring boneless red snapper in plantain leaves. For a change of pace, there are two French dishes: escargot and crepes stuffed with lobster. There's also a full bar with a long list of drink specials. On-site is a small budget guesthouse with 13 rooms.

Cuban

Metropol (Punta del Este Sur Court at the intersection of Carr. 3 and Carr. 194, 787/801-2877 or 787/801-2870, www.metropolpr.com, daily 11:30 A.M.–10:30 P.M., $9.95–35.95) is a modest casual restaurant serving excellent Cuban cuisine. The house special is *gallinita rellena de congri*—succulent roasted Cornish hen stuffed with a perfectly seasoned combination of rice and black beans. The presentation is no-nonsense and the service expedient.

INFORMATION AND SERVICES

Bank service is available at **Banco Popular** (Calle Garlinda Morales, between the central plaza and Carr. 3, 787/863-0101), which has an ATM. **Hospital San Pablo del Este** (Carr. 194 off Conquistador Ave., 787/863-0505) offers 24-hour emergency-room services. For pharmacy needs, there is a **Walgreens** (4302 Calle Marginal, 787/860-1600).

GETTING THERE AND GETTING AROUND

Although its airport has closed and relocated about 4 miles south to Ceiba, Fajardo is still a gateway to the nearby islands of Vieques and Culebra, thanks to daily ferry service and boats operating out of its seven marinas. Nevertheless, all the transportation options in Fajardo point in one direction: to Vieques, Culebra, or the Virgin Islands. Getting to Fajardo requires a flight into San Juan and either renting a car and driving there or taking a *publico,* a privately operated van transport service. **Padin** operates 24-hour transportation service between Fajardo and

the Luis Muñoz Marín International Airport in San Juan. Call Mrs. Rivera at 787/644-3091 (day) or 787/889-6202 (after 6 P.M.), or José Padin at 787/644-3091. The drive is about an hour.

By Air

The Fajardo airport has closed, and all operations have relocated about 4 miles south to the **Jose Aponte de la Torre Airport** (787/863-4447) on the former Roosevelt Roads Naval Base in Ceiba. It is a small operation devoted to servicing transportation to the coast's neighboring islands. **Isla Nena Air Service** (787/741-1577, www.islanena.8m.com) flies to Vieques, Culebra, and St. Thomas. **Vieques Air Link** (888/901-9247, www.viequesairlink.com) flies to Vieques, Culebra, and St. Croix. Charter air service is available through **Air Flamenco** (787/901-8256).

By Ferry

The Puerto Rican Port Authority operates daily ferry service to Vieques and Culebra from the Fajardo ferry terminal at Puerto Real (Carr. 195, 787/863-0705, or 787/863-4560).

The **passenger ferry** is primarily a commuter operation during the week and can often be crowded—especially on the weekends and holidays. Reservations are not accepted, but you can buy tickets in advance. Arrive no later than one hour before departure. Sometimes the ferry cannot accommodate everyone who wants to ride. The trip typically takes about an hour to travel to Vieques ($4 round-trip) and 1.5 hours to Culebra ($4.50). There is no ferry service between Vieques and Culebra.

Note that ferry schedule is subject to change.

- **Fajardo to Vieques:** Monday–Friday 9:30 A.M., 1 P.M., 4:30 P.M., 8 P.M.; Saturday–Sunday and Monday holidays 9 A.M., 3 P.M., 6 P.M.

- **Vieques to Fajardo:** Monday–Friday 6:30 A.M., 11 A.M., 3 P.M., 6 P.M.; Saturday–Sunday and Monday holidays 6:30 A.M., 1 P.M., 4:30 P.M.

- **Fajardo to Culebra:** Daily 9 A.M., 3 P.M., 7 P.M.

- **Culebra to Fajardo:** Daily 6:30 A.M., 1 P.M., 5 P.M.

There is also a weekday **cargo/car ferry** from Fajardo that goes between Culebra and Fajardo, for which reservations are required. But be aware that most car-rental agencies in Puerto Rico do not permit their automobiles to leave the main island. The best option is to leave your car in Fajardo and rent another car on Culebra. The trip usually takes about 2.5 hours, and the cost is $15 for small vehicles and $19 for large vehicles. The schedule is as follows:

- **Fajardo to Vieques:** Monday–Friday 4 A.M., 9:30 A.M., 4:30 P.M.

- **Vieques to Fajardo:** Monday 6 A.M., 1:30 P.M., 6 P.M.

- **Fajardo to Culebra:** Monday, Tuesday, and Thursday 4 A.M. and 4:30 P.M.; Wednesday and Friday 4 A.M., 9:30 A.M., 4:30 P.M.

- **Culebra to Fajardo:** Monday, Tuesday, and Thursday 7 A.M. and 6 P.M.; Wednesday and Friday 7 A.M., 1 P.M., 6 P.M.

Marinas

Fajardo's main commercial marina is **Marina Puerto Real** (Carr. 195, 787/863-2188). This is where the Puerto Rican Port Authority operates daily ferry service to Vieques and Culebra.

Other marinas include the tony **Villa Marina Yacht Harbour** (Carr. 987, km 1.3, Fajardo, 787/863-5131, fax 787/863-2320, gerente@villamarinapr.com, www.villa marinapr.com); **Puerto Del Rey** (Carr. 3, km 51.4, Fajardo, 809/860-1000 or 809/863-5792); and **Inversiones Isleta Marina** (787/643-2180, luisdiaz@coqui.net), offshore at Puerto Real Plaza, a startling high-rise development surrounded by ocean.

EAST COAST

Naguabo and Humacao

Check out the petite plaza with the umbrella-shaped trees in the town proper of Nagaubo, then go straight to its seaside community off Carretera 3. There's a slightly Mediterranean feel to this friendly little town, which overlooks a large bay and a hilly peninsula dotted with houses that cling to its sides. A long, wide *malécon*, a seawall with a balustrade, lines the ocean side of the road; shops, restaurants, and bars line the other side. Downtown Humacao is much more bustling with shops and restaurants clustered around a shady plaza flanked by a church and *alcadia* (town hall). But the main reason to go is to catch some rays at Balneario Santiago or to pamper yourself in the luxury of Palmas del Mar resort.

SIGHTS

Balneario Santiago (Carr. 3, km 72.4, Humacao, 787/852-1660 or 787/852-3066, Mon.–Fri. 7:30 A.M.–3:30 P.M., Sat.–Sun. and Mon. holidays 7:30 A.M.–5 P.M., $3 cars, $2 motorcycles, $4 vans, $5 buses, camping $25–40) is a great stretch of publicly maintained beach and vacation center with a swimming pool featuring a big waterslide, modest overnight accommodations, camping facilities, bathrooms, and picnic shelters. Adjacent to the balneario, along about km 68.3, is a large shady **wilderness beach** that is unfortunately heavily littered and crawling with feral dogs. On the weekends you can find vendors there selling beverages, trinkets, oysters, and other food items. From here you can see **Cayo Santiago,** also known as Monkey Island because of the large population of rhesus monkeys placed there for safekeeping by animal researchers. Visitors are not allowed on the island, but they're welcome to dive and snorkel around its edges and watch the primates from a distance.

Reserva Natural de Humacao (Carr. 3, km 74.3, Humacao, 787/852-6058, Mon.–Fri. 7:30 A.M.–3:30 P.M.; Sat.–Sun. and Mon. holidays 7:30 A.M.–6 P.M. May–Aug.; Sat.–Sun. and Mon. holidays 7:30 A.M.–5:30 P.M. Sept.–Apr., free) is a lovely natural reserve containing 3,186 acres of swamps, marshes, channels, and an interconnected lagoon system perfect for kayaking. There are also six miles of walking and bike trails. Sights along the way include an antique water-pumping station and bunkers constructed during World War II. Tour outfitters Water Sports & Ecotours operates out of the reserve, offering walking tours for $3.50 per person and kayak rentals for $10 per hour per person.

Iglesia Dulce Nombre de Jesus (3 Ave. Font Martelo, Humacao, 787/852-0868), located on the main plaza in downtown Humacao, is a Spanish colonial–style church built in 1793.

Museo Casa Roig (66 Calle Antonio Lopez, Humacao, 787/852-8380, fax 787/850-9144, www.uprh.edu/~museocr, Wed.–Fri. and Sun. 10 A.M.–4 P.M.) is a museum and cultural center operated by the University of Puerto Rico in Humacao. It was originally a private home built in 1919 by Antonin Nechodoma, a student of the Frank Lloyd Wright style of architecture.

SPORTS AND RECREATION

Palmas del Mar Country Club (Palmas del Mar, Country Club Dr., Humacao, 787/285-2255, www.palmasdelmar.com) has two 18-hole, 72-par courses: Golf Club was built in 1974 by Gary Player, and Flamboyan, considered one of the island's most challenging, is a newer course designed by Rees Jones. There are also tennis courts, an equestrian center, an enormous pool, a fitness center, and a modest spa.

Sea Ventures Palmas Dive Center (110 Harbour Dr., Palmas del Mar, Humacao, 787/781-8086 or 787/739-3483, seaventures@divepuertorico.com, www.divepalmasdelmar.com) offers daily two-tank dives in the morning and snorkeling trips in the afternoon. There are more than 35 dives sites in the area,

including overhangs, caverns, reefs, and tunnels. It also goes to Cayo Santiago.

Rancho Buena Vista (Palmas Dr., Palmas Del Mar Resort, Humacao, 787/479-7479, www.ranchobuenavistapr.com) is an equestrian center offering horseback riding on the beach and pony rides for children.

Water Sports & Ecotours (Reserva Natural de Humacao, Carr. 3, km 74.3, Humacao, 787/852-6058, Mon.–Fri. 7:30 A.M.–3:30 P.M.; Sat.–Sun. and Mon. holidays 7:30 A.M.–6 P.M. May–Aug.; Sat.–Sun. and Mon. holidays 7:30 A.M.–5:30 P.M. Sept.–Apr.) offers walking tours for $3.50 per person and kayak rental for $10 per hour per person in the 3,186-acre reserve.

ENTERTAINMENT

Casino Real at Palmas de Mar (Four Points By Sheraton, 170 Candelero Dr., Palmas del Mar, 787/850-6000, daily 10 A.M.–2 A.M.) is a modest 7,000-square-foot casino with slot machines, blackjack, roulette, and Texas hold 'em.

ACCOMMODATIONS

Palmas del Mar (Carr. 3, km 86.4, Humacao, 787/852-8888, www.palmasdelmar.com) is a 2,700-acre planned community that includes residential and resort developments. **Sheraton Four Points Hotel & Casino** (170 Candelero Dr., Humacao, 787/850-6000, fax 787/850-6001, www.starwoodhotels.com, $240–314 s/d) operates the 107-room hotel, featuring all the amenities one would expect from a Sheraton. Attractions include more than three miles of beach, a casino, an 8,000-square-foot pool, a 200-slip marina, two golf courses, tennis courts, a fitness center, a spa, an equestrian center, and 18 restaurants. For vacation rentals in Palmas del Mar, visit www.prwest.com. Police, fire, postal, banking, and medical services are all available at Palmas del Mar.

◀ **Casa Cubuy Eco Lodge** (Carr. 191, km 22, Naguabo, 787/874-6221, fax 787/874-4316, www.casacubuy.com, $90–115 s/d plus 9 percent tax, includes breakfast, 2-night minimum) is a small low-key lodge on the quiet, less visited southern side of El Yunque. Perched on a hill above a gurgling stream, this is definitely the place to go to get away from it all. Amenities are few (no TV!) beyond balconies and hammocks. But you're a short hike away from waterfalls and a natural pool where you can take an invigorating dip. You can buy sack lunches for $7, and dinner is served if six or more guests request it by 1 P.M. ($18 per person). In-room massages are available.

Centro Vacacional de Humacao Villas Punta Santiago (Carr. 3, km 72.4, Punta Santiago, Humacao, 787/622-5200, www .parquesnacionalespr.com, $65–71 cabanas, $109–115 villas, 2-night minimum) is a government-maintained and operated vacation center patronized almost exclusively by Puerto Ricans but open to anyone looking for basic economical accommodations on the ocean. The gated property features a yellow-and-adobe-colored complex containing 99 cabanas and villas. Only the villas are air-conditioned, but both cabanas and villas have full kitchens. Linens, towels, and cooking utensils are not provided. Amenities include tennis courts, a playground, a pool with a waterslide, and lovely shady grounds featuring almond trees, palms, and *flamboyans*.

FOOD

Chez Daniel (Palmas del Mar, Anchor's Village Marina, Humacao, 787/850-3838, fax 787/285-2330, chezdaniel@libertypr.net, www.chezdanielpalmasdelmar.com, Wed.–Sun. 6:30–10 P.M., closed June, $27–35) is an award-winning upscale fine-dining restaurant serving French cuisine with a Caribbean twist. Grilled duck breast, bouillabaisse, and Dover sole are among its specialties. It also has an extensive wine list. Dine inside or outside overlooking the marina. Check out the massive Sunday brunch buffet ($42 per person).

Los Makos Restaurant (Carr. 3, Nagaubo Playa, Naguabo, 787/874-2353, Tues.–Wed. 11:30 A.M.–8 P.M., Thurs. and Sun. 11 A.M.–10 P.M., Fri.–Sat. 11 A.M.–midnight, $10–40) is a large modern restaurant with dining indoors and out, and a separate bar. It specializes in seafood, and its big seller by far is the local lobster, served in salads, soups, creole sauce, charbroiled, in garlic butter, or "Makos" style, accompanied by octopus, conch, and shrimp.

EAST COAST

Yabucoa, Maunabo, and Patillas

Often bypassed by visitors, Yabucoa, Maunabo, and Patillas are quiet, low-key, seaside municipalities in the southeastern corner of Puerto Rico that offer a tranquil getaway from the crowds, traffic, and American influence found elsewhere on the island. Nevertheless, the area is home to several small well-maintained hotels and restaurants that serve travelers who aren't looking for a lot of excitement or nightlife.

Unlike the island's southwestern corner, the vegetation here is emerald-green thanks to the convergence of several rivers from the Cordillera Central. In Maunabo, the Cordillera Central descends into the Caribbean Ocean, creating lovely views where the mountains meet the sea. Maunabo was once the domain of Carib Indians and pirates, but along with Patillas, it is primarily an agricultural community today, producing everything from cattle to grapes. Yabucoa was once integral to Puerto Rico's sugar production during the industry's heyday. At one time it had six sugar mills in operation. Today it is a manufacturing center, producing electronics, clothing, and cigarettes. Unfortunately, it's also home to an unsightly oil refinery that mars the view of its coast.

SIGHTS

The primary reason to visit the area is for its long stretches and private pockets of deserted beaches gently lapped by the Caribbean Sea. The most popular one is **Playa Punta Tuna**

(Carr. 760, km 3, Maunabo), where the low-lying hills of the Cordillera Central kiss the sea. In addition to a nice wide mile-long beach and great surfing, this is where you'll find picturesque Faro de Punta Tuna, a lighthouse perched atop a hilly point that juts into the water.

Other beaches in Maunabo are **Los Bohíos** (Carr. 760, Bordaleza), which offers a wonderful view of the Punta Tuna lighthouse and great surfing, and **Los Pinos** (Carr. 901), northwest of Playa Punta Tuna. **Playa Lucia** (Carr. 901, km 4) is a small beach in Yabucoa.

Faro de Punta Tuna (follow the signs from Carr. 760, Maunabo, 787/861-0301, Wed.–Sun. 9 A.M.–4 P.M., free) is a neoclassical-style lighthouse built in 1863. Stop by the office for information on the history of the lighthouse and the surrounding community, available in English and Spanish, then stroll the shady 0.25-mile path toward the octagonal tower high on a cliff offering 180-degree views of the ocean and mountains.

ENTERTAINMENT AND EVENTS

If you want something to do besides loll around on the beach all day, visit during festival time when things get lively. In Maunabo, the big draw is **Festival Jueyero,** a celebration that fetes the land crab, held in late September in the town plaza on Calle Santiago Iglesia. All sorts of crab dishes are on the menu, as are a parade, crab races, and more. Maunabo is also home to **Fiestas del Pueblo,** a town celebration held in late June in the plaza featuring music, dance, rides, games, and food kiosks. Yabucoa has a **Patron Saint Festival,** held in late September through early October in Parque Felix Millan, to commemorate Saint Angeles Custodios.

ACCOMMODATIONS

Hotel Parador Palmas de Lucia (Carr. 901 at Carr. 9911, Playa Lucia, Yabucoa, 787/893-4423, www.tropicalinnspr.com, $119 s/d, includes breakfast and snacks) is a modern motel-style property with a petite pool and a small

sandy beach half a block away. It has 34 simple, comfortable rooms featuring air-conditioning, satellite TV, refrigerators, microwaves, coffeemakers, and balconies. There's a restaurant on-site serving breakfast, lunch, and dinner.

◖ **Lucia Beach Villas** (Carr. 99011 at Carr. 901, Yabucoa, 787/266-1111 or 787/266-1716, www.luciabeachvillas.com, $152 for 2 people, $185 for 4, $250 for 6) is a newly constructed, modern townhouse-style complex of 15 connected units located in a remote spot where you can see the mountains meet the sea. The two-story units with loft-style bedrooms feature air-conditioning, satellite TV, Wi-Fi, full kitchens, 1.5 baths, and a pool with a dramatic backdrop that features a natural waterfall that trickles down the mountain behind it. Each unit sleeps up to six people. There's no restaurant on-site, but a secluded public beach is located right across the street.

Costa del Mar Guest House (Carr. 901, km 5.6, Yabucoa, 787/266-6276 or 787/893-6374, fax 787/893-6374, www.tropicalinnspr.com, 2-night stay $359 for 2 people, $55 for 3, and $570 for 4, includes breakfast) is a new property with 16 units, 12 of which overlook the ocean (although there is no beach access). Amenities include air-conditioning, satellite TV, balconies, a pool, and a basketball court.

◖ **Caribe Playa Beach Resort** (Carr. 3, km 112, Patillas, 787/839-6339, fax 787/839-1817, www.caribeplaya.com, $130 s/d plus tax) is a bit of a misnomer. It's too small, modest, and low-key to qualify for what most people think of when they think of a resort. Instead, it is quaintly old-fashioned, intimate, casual, and quiet. The pale yellow and white motel-style structure hugs the coastline so closely that you can practically hear the waves lapping the beach from the bed. The 27 units are simply furnished and come with air-conditioning, satellite TV, refrigerators, and coffee makers. Wi-Fi is available in common areas. The grounds are lushly landscaped and appointed with grills, shady hammocks, umbrella tables, and lounge chairs. The seaside Ocean View Terrace serves three meals a day.

Parador Caribbean Paradise (Carr. 3, km

114.3, Patillas, 787/839-5885, fax 787/271-0069, www.caribbeanparadisepr.com, $80–99) is a motel-style facility with 24 rooms. Rooms come with air-conditioning, cable TV, and a coffeemaker. Amenities include a swimming pool, tennis courts, and basketball courts.

FOOD

Gemelo y Su Rumba (Carr. 981, km 4.3, Yabucoa, 787/585-6284, Mon.–Thurs. 9 A.M.–9 P.M., Fri.–Sun. 9 A.M.–midnight, $1–18) is a casual open-air bar and restaurant serving exceptional empanadas during the week and fresh fish specials Thursday through Sunday. The owner, Leftie, is a musician, and he turns the place into a lively music venue on Sundays when crowds flock there for the live salsa music and dancing that goes on throughout the day.

Restaurante El Nuevo Horizonte (Carr. 901, km 8.8, Yabucoa, 787/893-5492, fax 787/893-3768, Wed.–Thurs. 11 A.M.–8 P.M., Fri.–Sat. 11 A.M.–10 P.M., Sun. 11 A.M.–8 P.M., $12.95–28.95) offers inside dining on seafood and Puerto Rican cuisine while enjoying the ocean view from high up on a mountain peak. Outside is a kiosk serving empanadas and other Puerto Rican–style fritters and beers.

Palmas de Lucia (Hotel Parador Palmas de Lucia, Carr. 901 at Carr. 9911, Playa Lucia, Yabucoa, 787/893-4423, www.tropicalinnspr .com, Sun.–Thurs. 8 A.M.–9 P.M., Fri.–Sat. 8 A.M.–10 P.M., $11–17) serves three meals a day. Lunch consists of burgers, ribs, and chicken fingers, but dinner specializes in a variety of fresh seafood, including halibut, shrimp, and lobster, as well as Puerto Rican dishes such as *mofongo* and *asopao*.

AquaMar Steakhouse & Seafood (Carr. 901, km 1.7, Maunabo, 787/861-1363, Mon.–Wed. 11 A.M.–10 P.M., Thurs.–Sun. 11 A.M.–11 P.M., $12–34) is a contemporary, dressy-casual restaurant serving Angus and Kobe beef, seafood, pasta, and exotic meats, including ostrich, buffalo, and boar. It also boasts a large selection of wines.

Café Terraza Panaderia y Respoteria (11 Ave. Calimano, Maunabo, 787/861-3375, daily 7 A.M.–11 P.M., $2–5) serves everything you could want, from whole baked chickens and Puerto Rican cuisine to pastries and sandwiches. There is also a small market selling cold drinks and dry goods.

Los Bohios (Carr. 760, km 2.3, Maunabo, 787/861-2545, Wed.–Sun., $10–18) is a casual open-air restaurant overlooking the ocean that serves Puerto Rican cuisine, seafood, and steaks.

Open daily and serving three meals a day is the small seaside **Ocean View Terrace** (at Caribe Playa Beach Resort, Carr. 3, km 112, Patillas, 787/839-6339, fax 787/839-1817, www.caribeplaya.com, daily 8 A.M.–10:30 A.M., noon–3 P.M., and 6–9:30 P.M., reservations required for dinner, $14–19), which specializes in continental and Puerto Rican cuisine. The menu includes pasta, whole fried snapper, and *mofongo*.

EAST COAST

VIEQUES AND CULEBRA

Vieques and Culebra are two island municipalities a mere 8 and 17 miles, respectively, off the east coast of Puerto Rico, but the lifestyle there is light-years away from that of the main island. Referred to as the Spanish Virgin Islands, Vieques and Culebra are often described as "the way Puerto Rico used to be." The pace of life doesn't just slow down, it comes to a screeching halt. There are no fast-food restaurants or high-rise hotels, no golf courses or casinos, virtually no nightlife, and few tourist sights. And the only way to reach the islands is by plane or ferry. But what they do have are stunning beaches, world-class water sports, and lots of opportunity for R&R.

The small Spanish fort and museum **El Fortín Conde de Mirasol** on Vieques and the **Museo Histórica de Culebra** are the closest things to cultural attraction the islands have to offer. Instead, one of the main reasons to go are the islands' wide sandy beaches, the most popular being **Balneario Sun Bay** in Vieques and **Playa Flamenco** in Culebra. In addition to its beaches, Culebra and Vieques offer fantastic opportunities for diving and snorkeling. If you don't want to go on a group tour, excellent snorkeling from the beach at Playa Carlos Rosario in Culebra is easily accessible. And visitors to Vieques would be remiss not to visit the bioluminescent **Mosquito Bay,** which requires an overnight stay.

PLANNING YOUR TIME

To get to Vieques and Culebra, you can fly from Ceiba or San Juan or take a ferry from

© JIM JOHNSON

HIGHLIGHTS

◖ **El Fortín Conde de Mirasol:** Tour the last fort built by colonial Spain and see the 4,000-year-old remains of a man exhumed from an archaeological site in Vieques (page 82).

◖ **Mosquito Bay:** Take a guided kayak or electric pontoon boat to Vieques's bioluminescent bay, where you can get up close and personal with the water that glows an electric blue at night (page 83).

◖ **Balneario Sun Bay:** Vieques's mile-long, sandy, crescent-shaped beach on crystal-blue waters comes with bathroom, shower, and snack-bar facilities (page 84).

◖ **Playa Flamenco:** Puerto Rico's most celebrated stretch of white sand and aquamarine water is in Culebra. It's considered one of the most beautiful beaches in the United States (page 96).

◖ **Diving in Culebra:** Culebra is surrounded by 50 dive sites, and excellent snorkeling can be found right off its beaches. One of the best sites is Playa Carlos Rosario, which features a long coral reef rich with sea life (page 98).

LOOK FOR ◖ TO FIND RECOMMENDED SIGHTS, ACTIVITIES, DINING, AND LODGING.

Fajardo. If you're visiting for only a day or two, spring for the airfare to save time.

Although it's possible to get to your hotel and some of the islands' beaches using *publicos* (shared vans that carry multiple fares at a time), to fully explore the islands' remote beaches a rental car is recommended. Book early though, because they go fast.

Vieques and Culebra are such small islands that it's possible to spend a day and a night on each one to get a cursory feel for them both. But the reason most people go is to experience the islands' unparalleled natural beauty and soak up plenty of R&R. To do those things properly, it takes a few days to reset your internal clock to "island time" and achieve a blissful state of total relaxation.

HISTORY

Although details are sketchy, Vieques is believed to have been inhabited by a series of indigenous peoples possibly thousands of years before Christopher Columbus "discovered" Puerto Rico in 1493. Based on the discovery of remains found in Vieques, some historians date the earliest inhabitants to the Stone Age era more than 3,500 years ago.

Thanks to a few archaeological digs in Vieques, slightly more is known about the Saladoids, believed to have come from Venezuela around 250 B.C. They were followed by the Ostionoids around 400 B.C. and eventually the Taínos, a highly developed society of agriculturalists who lived on both Vieques and Culebra. The Taínos ruled Puerto Rico from about A.D. 1200 until the Spanish colonists wiped them out in the 1500s.

In the early 1500s, two Taíno brothers in Vieques journeyed to mainland Puerto Rico to help their fellow natives fight the Spanish conquerors. As a result, the governor of Puerto Rico sent troops to Vieques, where all the Taínos were killed or enslaved. For a long time after that, the islands became lawless havens for pirates who sought refuge in its protected harbors and ambushed passing ships.

In 1832 a Frenchman named Le Guillou, known as the founder of Vieques, arrived on the island. Under order of the governor of Puerto Rico, he restored order to the island and helped launch a golden era of prosperity. He brought over other Frenchmen from Guadeloupe and Martinique who established sugarcane plantations and processing plants that exported the products to Spain. The operations were manned by hundreds of slaves from Africa and thousands of free workers from surrounding islands. In the early 1800s, the area around Esperanza was a thriving community with an opera house, a movie theater, and a cultural center. But as the town tried to expand to accommodate its growing population, difficulty in clearing the thick vegetation led leaders to relocate the town center to Isabel Segunda in 1844. Vieques continued to enjoy

its prosperity until around 1880, when the sugar industry began to decline because of the development of cheaper sources elsewhere.

It was around this time that Culebra was being settled in fits and starts. The first attempt was in 1875 by a black Englishman named Stevens, who was named governor and given the task of protecting the island's waters from pirates. Later that same year he was assassinated. He was followed in 1880 by a Spaniard, Cayetano Escudero Sanz, who established the first settlement, called San Ildefonso. The island's sole economy was agriculture.

Upon the ratification in 1898 of the Treaty of Paris, which ended the Spanish-American War, Vieques and Culebra came under the rule of the U.S. government. During World War II, the U.S. military became the major landholder on both islands and began to use them for bomb practice and defense-testing sites. Protests begun in Culebra in 1971 led the United States to abandon operations in 1975. But Vieques toughed through 24 more years until a civilian was accidentally killed by a bomb in 1999. Several years of persistent protesting followed, which captured international attention and led to the incarceration of many activists. In 2003 the military abandoned its operations in Vieques. But its legacy lives on, some say, in the island's extraordinarily high rate of cancer.

Vieques

Vieques stands squarely in the nexus of a cultural crossroads. Just 25 miles long and 5 miles wide, it is a rustic, slow-paced island where horses roam freely and going to the beach is just about the only thing to do, at least for now.

In 2003, the Pentagon conceded and the Navy withdrew from Vieques. Its land—15,000 acres on the east side, along with 3,100 acres on the west side that was ceded two years earlier—was handed over to the federal Fish and Wildlife Service, which has classified the property a National Wildlife Refuge. Much of

the land is still off-limits while the Navy continues to clear it of contaminants and unexploded artillery, but so far two natural jewels, Red Beach and Blue Beach, on former Camp Garcia have been opened to visitors.

With the Navy gone, Vieques is on the verge of a tourism explosion. Although efforts are under way to ensure new development doesn't overwhelm the island's natural beauty, it's nearly certain that the sleepy, old-fashioned way of life will be affected.

The east and west ends of the island are still mostly off-limits to civilians, and the island's commercial districts are in the middle of the island. There are two communities, Isabel Segunda on the north coast and Esperanza on the south coast. **Isabel Segunda** is a small, traditional, but fairly charmless Puerto Rican town. Perhaps once the renovation of the plaza is completed, that will change. Many of the island's services lie within its 20 or so blocks, including the only gas stations and ATM. This is also where the ferry docks, and the airport is nearby.

Esperanza is more geared toward tourism. It's largely a residential area with a small strip of guesthouses and restaurants that line the coast overlooking the *malécon,* a picturesque sea walk rimmed by a balustrade. Two of the best reasons to visit Vieques are here: **Sun Bay,** one of the most beautiful public beaches in all of Puerto Rico, and **Mosquito Bay,** one of the world's most spectacular bioluminescent lagoons. Esperanza is also home to quite a few U.S. expatriates, many of whom came for a visit and couldn't bear to leave.

Aside from its gorgeous fine-sand beaches,

coral reefs, and mangrove bays, inland Vieques is mostly thick hilly forest and arid, barren stretches of desertlike land. Bats are said to be the only animal native to Vieques, but other wildlife commonly found includes geckos, iguanas, frogs, deer, pelicans, seagulls, egrets, herons, doves, and, of course, horses. Horses are a common mode of transportation in Vieques, and they follow the same traffic laws as automobiles, stopping at four-way stops, and so on. But they also graze and roam freely. The waters around the island are home to several endangered animals, including the manatee and sea turtles.

Accommodations on Vieques tend to be either small luxurious inns or bare-bones guesthouses. Few rooms have TVs or telephones—even the high-end ones. Several interesting restaurants serving international and Caribbean cuisine have opened in recent years. Nearly every business accepts credit cards, unless otherwise noted, and it's a good thing: Vieques is not inexpensive. Because nearly every commodity must be shipped in, prices

A lovely blue and white balustrade lines the *malecón* in Esperanza.

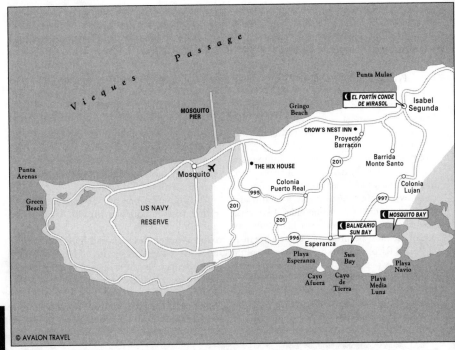

Vieques Passage

Punta Mulas

MOSQUITO PIER

Gringo Beach

[EL FORTÍN CONDE DE MIRASOL   Isabel Segunda

CROW'S NEST INN •   Proyecto Barracon

Mosquito ✈   • THE HIX HOUSE

201

Barrida Monte Santo

Punta Arenas

Green Beach

US NAVY RESERVE

995   Colonia Puerto Real

997   Colonia Lujan

201

[MOSQUITO BAY

201

[BALNEARIO SUN BAY

996   Esperanza

Playa Esperanza

Sun Bay

Playa Navio

Cayo Afuera

Cayo de Tierra

Playa Media Luna

© AVALON TRAVEL

for everything from accommodations to meals rival those in San Juan. Many businesses close on Mondays and during the low-season summer months. Even during the high season, posted business hours may be more of a suggestion than reality. It's always a good idea to call first.

There are occasional water shortages on the island, and plumbing can be a bit of an issue. Signs in public restrooms request that toilet paper be discarded in wastepaper baskets instead of flushed. There are also occasional gasoline shortages, especially on weekends.

Vieques is home to 10,000 inhabitants, and it reportedly has one of the highest unemployment rates in the United States. It's not surprising that petty theft from parked cars is a continuing problem. When in town, visitors are encouraged to keep their cars locked at all times and never to leave anything in them. The greatest threat to car break-ins is at the beach, where culprits use a smash-and-grab tactic.

Drivers are encouraged to leave all the windows rolled down and the sunroof and glove box open to avoid having to pay the cost of replacing a broken window. And always park your car as close to you as possible—preferably away from any bushes and within sight range.

Except for a couple of late-night watering holes, there's little nightlife in Vieques. Since most accommodations don't have TVs and the restaurants typically close by 10 P.M., the best option is just to go to bed so you can hit the beaches early the next day.

With the Navy gone, Vieques is teetering on the cusp of a new era. If you want to see it in its pristine glory, you'd better go soon.

SIGHTS
[El Fortín Conde de Mirasol
Built between 1845 and 1855, El Fortín Conde de Mirasol (Fort Count Mirasol, Carr. 989, Isabel Segunda, 787/741-1717, www.enchanted-isle.com/elfortin/index

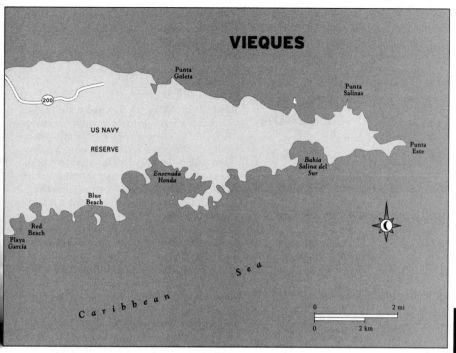

.htm, Wed.–Sun. 10 A.M.–4 P.M.) was the last fort built by the Spanish in the New World. Never attacked or used in battle, it originally housed Spanish troops and later became a jail and execution site. Among those incarcerated here were fugitive slaves from local sugar plantations and political prisoners who sought Puerto Rico's independence from Spain. Later it was used as a municipal jail until the 1940s, when it was closed and fell into disrepair. In 1989 the Institute of Puerto Rico began restoration of the fort, which still has its original brick floors, exterior walls, and hardwood beams. Today the fort is home to the **Vieques Museum of Art and History,** home of Hombre de Puerto Ferro, the 4,000-year-old remains of a man whose body was discovered in an archaeological site near Esperanza, as well as exhibits dedicated to the island's indigenous people, its historic sugarcane industry, and local artists. It also contains the Vieques Historic Archives.

Often referred to as Vieques Stonehenge, the archaeological site of **Hombre de Puerto Ferro** is on the south side of the island off Carretera 997. About 0.25 mile east of the entrance to Sun Bay, turn inland onto a dirt road that takes you to the fenced-off site. Giant boulders mark the spot where the remains were excavated in 1990. Some believe the boulders were placed around the grave; others say it's a natural phenomenon.

Mosquito Bay

Mosquito Bay (off Carr. 997, near Esperanza, 787/741-0800) is the site of Vieques's celebrated bioluminescent bay, and no trip to the island is complete without a visit. Inside the Balneario Sun Bay complex, Mosquito Bay is a protected wildlife refuge not only because its fragile mangrove ecosystem is vital to the island's environmental health but also because it contains one of the most robust bioluminescent bays in the world. Harmless single-celled dinoflagellates that inhabit the warm water light up

ISABEL SEGUNDA

(Map labels:)

Passage

Vieques

CASA LA LANCHITA

BRAVO BEACH HOTEL

CALLE NORTH SHORE

PUNTA MULAS LIGHTHOUSE ★

FISHERMAN'S PIER

FERRY DOCK

CALLE PLINIO PETERSON

AL'S MAR AZUL ▼   MAMASONGA

CALLE BENÍTEZ GUZMAN

BALDORIOTY DE CASTRO

TOURISM OFFICE ■

C MUÑOZ RIVERA

BANCO POPULAR ■

CALLE LEBRÓN

POST OFFICE ■

CALLE QUERO

CAFÉ MEDIA LUNA ▼

EL FORTÍN CONDE DE MIRASOL ★

CALLE JOSÉ G. MELLADO

CALLE ANTONIO G. QUIÑONES

▼ TROPICAL BABY CAFÉ

▼ RICHARD'S CAFÉ

0   200 yds
0   200 m

POLICE STATION ■
To Airport (200)   (997)   To Esperanza

© AVALON TRAVEL

the bay with an electric blue glow when they sense motion.

There are several outfitters in Vieques that provide night excursions on kayaks or an electric pontoon boat for an up-close experience with the phenomenon. For best results, plan your trip during a new moon, when the bay glows brightest.

Other Sights

Built in the late 1800s, **El Faro Punta Mulas** (Calle Plinio Peterson, north of Isabel Segunda, 787/741-0060) looks less like a lighthouse and more like a modest, rectangular government building with a large light on top of it. It's still operational today. Entry is not permitted.

The small **Vieques Conservation and Historic Trust** (138 Calle Flamboyan, Esperanza, 787/741-8850, daily 8 A.M.–4 P.M., gift shop 11 A.M.–4 P.M.) contains modest ecological and archaeological exhibits.

BEACHES

Aside from Mosquito Bay, the main reason to come to Vieques is to enjoy the staggering beauty of its miles of remote, pristine beaches and clear, turquoise waters. Each beach has its own unique characteristics—some are calm and shallow, others have big crashing waves, and still others offer spectacular snorkeling. Several are accessible only from dirt trails, off road or by foot.

Although violent crime is uncommon in Vieques, the island has a petty theft problem, which can be avoided if you use caution. Be vigilant around beaches with bushes where culprits may hide. Never take anything of value to the beach, including digital cameras or personal ID. If someone can't watch your things while you swim, bring a "dry bag," available at dive shops, to contain a car key and a photocopy of your driver's license. Don't leave anything inside your car and be sure to roll all your windows down and open the glove box so it's apparent nothing is inside.

◖ Balneario Sun Bay

The island's best beaches are on the southern coast. The most spectacular is the long white crescent and calm waters of Balneario Sun Bay (Sombé) (Carr. 997, east of Esperanza, 787/741-8198, daily 9 A.M.–5 P.M., $2). It's the only publicly maintained beach in Vieques. Surrounded by a tall cyclone fence, it has plenty of modern, fairly clean facilities, including bathrooms, showers, changing rooms, a snack bar, and guards. Camping is permitted for $10 a day, reservations required (787/741-8198). Adding to the charm of the place is the herd of horses that grazes here.

The Balneario Sun Bay complex also encompasses two smaller, more secluded beaches farther eastward along a sandy road. The first one you'll encounter is **Media Luna**, a

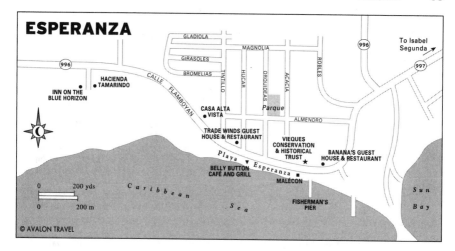

ESPERANZA

protective cove where the water is shallow. Farther eastward is **Navio Beach,** which sometimes has large waves and is popular with gay beachgoers.

Other Beaches

If you want something remote and untamed, venture onto the former Camp Garcia to get to **Red Beach** and **Blue Beach** (daily 6 A.M.–6 P.M.). Traveling south on Carretera 997, turn left at the sign onto a dirt road about halfway between Isabel Segunda and Esperanza. Follow the signs past the old Navy airstrip and turn right to reach Red Beach, or continue about two more miles and then fork right to arrive at Blue Beach.

On the extreme western end of the island is **Green Beach,** at the end of a dirt road off Carretera 200 (look for the 300-year-old ceiba tree with the massive trunk along the way). It features a narrow strip of sand punctuated by coral outcroppings and a view of the main island. There's good snorkeling to be found here, and lots of starfish to be discovered in the shallow waters along Laguna Kiani, on the north shore as you head eastward from Punta Arenas. But whatever you do, don't stay on Green Beach past about 4 P.M. because that's when the tiny, voracious sand gnats descend.

Esperanza Beach is a fairly unremarkable beach along that community's strip of restaurants and guesthouses. But it's within walking distance if you're staying in town and offers excellent snorkeling, especially around Cayo Afuera, a tiny islet just offshore.

SPORTS AND RECREATION
Mosquito Bay Tours

Any trip to Vieques would be incomplete without a trip to the bioluminescent Mosquito Bay unless, of course, you visit during a full moon, when the ambient light diminishes the visibility of the bioluminescent organisms that light up the water.

Island Adventures (787/741-0720, biobay@ biobay.com, www.biobay.com, $25) operates a well-run tour of the bay that lasts about 2.5 hours and starts with a short bilingual lecture. Then guests are bused to Mosquito Bay, where they board an electric pontoon boat that tools around the electric-blue water. Guides are exceedingly friendly and informative. You'll also get a lesson on the constellations. As if that weren't enough, free pickup and drop-off service is provided along Calle Flamboyan in Esperanza.

If you want a more up-close and personal tour of the bay, **Blue Caribe Kayaks** (149 Calle Flamboyan, Esperanza, 787/741-2522) provides kayak tours of Mosquito Bay for $30 per person.

JOURNEY THROUGH THE ELECTRIC-BLUE WATERS OF MOSQUITO BAY

The evening starts at twilight with a bumpy ride through Esperanza in a rattly old school bus. The driver for Island Adventures motors along the seaside strip picking up adventurous patrons of all stripes along the way.

My fellow voyagers include an older couple and their adult daughter, a young family with two inquisitive little boys, a pregnant woman and her husband, and a half dozen rambunctious 20-somethings, whose high spirits suggest they've just left a nearby bar.

We arrive at the Island Adventures headquarters, a converted two-story house with a small office downstairs where we buy our tickets and peruse a small selection of T-shirts and postcards. We're instructed to go upstairs for a brief lecture. There we join others who had forgone the free pickup service and driven themselves.

The room resembles an elementary school science lab. Small tables and chairs fill the back of the room, bookshelves are lined with marine biology texts, and instructional posters fill the walls. Once everyone is assembled, we receive a child-friendly lecture, explaining just why the bioluminescent lagoon in Mosquito Bay glows.

The mangrove bay's rich nutrients and clean warm water create the perfect environment for sustaining the zillions of dinoflagellates that wash into the bay during high tide and remain trapped there when the tide recedes. The microscopic single-celled creature is unique in several ways. For one, it contains properties similar to both plants and animals. But more notably, when it senses motion, it experiences a chemical reaction that creates a burst of light not unlike that of a firefly.

Puerto Rico is said to have as many as seven bays rich in dinoflagellates, although only three are commonly known: Phosphorescent Bay in La Parguera on the southwest coast of Puerto Rico, Laguna Grande in Fajardo on the east coast, and Mosquito Bay in Vieques. Mosquito Bay is touted as one of the most spectacular bioluminescent bays in the world because of its high concentration of dinoflagellates and the absence of pollution and ambient light. Because darkness is required to see the glow, the best nights to tour the bay are when no moon is visible.

After our lecture we pile back into the bus and bounce our way over the rutted roads inside Balneario Sun Bay to reach Mosquito Bay Nature Reserve. Tonight is a new moon, and no matter how hard we peer out the windows, all we see is blackness. The bus pulls all the way up to the water's edge, where several guides and the boat captain await our arrival, and we unload, clutching our cameras and bug spray. A ramp appears from no where, and we walk across it to find our places on the bench seats that run along both sides of the electric pontoon boat.

Silently we motor across the calm waters into the dark lagoon. The sky is filled with constellations, which our guides point out and identify by name. We notice that the lip of the boat's wake looks an eerie pale blue. Then someone stomps loudly several times on the floor of the boat, and we see scores of blue zigzags radiating away from us – the underwater wakes of fish fleeing our path.

As we venture deeper into the lagoon, the night grows darker while the electric-blue glow of the water becomes more vivid.

Before April 2007, when the Department of Natural Resources banned swimming in the island's bioluminescent bays, the climax of the trip came when visitors were permitted to jump in and frolic in the bathtub-warm water, where they could swim, turn flips, and create water angels in the electric-blue drink. Now we must content ourselves with watching the boat's blue wake and spotting electric fish trails through the water. It's still a magical experience, but it's not quite the same.

After we motor back to shore and file onto the bus, we return to town in silence as everyone seems lost in thought. The bus makes intermittent stops in front of the crowded bars, restaurants, and guesthouses that line the strip in Esperanza. One at a time, we disembark and go our separate ways to eat dinner, have a few drinks, and marvel at the wonder of our nighttime journey through the electric-blue waters of Mosquito Bay.

Kayak rentals are also available for $10–15 per hour, $25–35 for four hours, and $45–55 all day. Snorkeling-equipment rentals are also available.

Snorkeling, Diving, and Fishing

The best diving in Vieques can be found along the fringe reefs on the southern side of the island. **Nan-Sea Charters** (787/741-2390, dgephoto1@aol.com, www.nanseacharters.com) offers half-day, two-dive trips starting at $100 from a 28-foot dive boat. One-tank shore dives are $50. Custom coral tours and diving certification courses are also available.

Combine a day of sailing and snorkeling with **Sail Vieques** in Isabel Segunda (787/508-7245, billwillo@yahoo.com). A half-day trip with snorkeling is $50, and a daylong trip to the southern tip of the Bermuda Triangle with snorkeling is $110. Captain Bill also offers a two-hour sunset cruise for $30.

Vieques Adventure Company (69 Calle Orquideas, Esperanza, 787/692-9162, garry@ciequesadventures.com, www.bikevieques.com) offers kayak rentals ($45) and tours, as well as individual kayak fishing tours ($150).

Go inshore fishing for kingfish, amberjack, barracuda, pompano, and tarpon on a 21-foot Ranger bay boat with Captain Franco Gonzalez of **Caribbean Fly Fishing** (61 Calle Orquideas, Esperanza, 787/741-1337 or 787/450-3744, flyfish@coqui.net, www.viequesflyfishing.com).

Mountain Biking

Landlubbers looking to explore inland Vieques can get a guided, off-the-beaten-path mountain-bike tour with **Vieques Adventure Company** (69 Calle Orquideas, Esperanza, 787/692-9162, garry@ciequesadventures.com, www.bikevieques.com). Bikes rent for $35 a day ($25 a day for multiple days) and include a helmet, a lock, and a trail repair kit. Half-day tours are $75. Combination bike-kayak-snorkel tours are also available.

ENTERTAINMENT AND EVENTS
Cockfights

If there is such a thing as politically correct cockfighting, it exists in Vieques, where the birds do not fight until death. Winners are proclaimed by judges before the birds are seriously harmed. Fights are held at **Gallera Puerto Real** (Carr. 200, about three miles west of Isabel Segunda, no telephone), typically on Friday nights and Sunday afternoons, although the schedule changes. Admission is $10; women admitted free. Food and alcohol are served.

Bars

If partying into the wee hours is your idea of the perfect vacation, Vieques may not be the place for you. There are no nightclubs, discos, or casinos on the island, and many of the restaurants close by 10 P.M. There are a couple of watering holes that stay open late, though. Salty sea dogs gravitate to the no-frills **Banana's Beach Bar and Grill** (Calle Flamboyan, Esperanza, 787/741-8700, bananasvieques@gmail.com, www.bananasguesthouse.com, Sun.–Thurs. until 1 A.M., Fri. until 2 A.M.). A sign behind the bar proudly proclaims: "This Is A Gin-u-wine Sleazy Waterfront Bar." Ask the bartender what the drink special is, and she's likely to respond: "A beer and a shot." But it also serves a potent rum punch made with three kinds of rum. There are eight small guest rooms on-site if you drink too much and can't drive home.

Apologies to Banana's, but the real "gin-u-wine sleazy waterfront bar" in Vieques is **Al's Mar Azul** (577 Calle Plinio Peterson, Isabel Segunda, 787/741-3400, Sun.–Thurs. 11 A.M.–1 A.M., Fri.–Sat. 11 A.M.–2:30 A.M.). Hanging right over the water, this pleasant dive bar is cluttered with a random collection of junk that looks as if it has been sitting around the place for decades: old lifesaving rings, an inflated blowfish, paper lanterns, the grill off a jeep, a huge plastic turtle, a carved coconut head. It doesn't serve food, but someone will call your order in and pick it up for you at Mamasonga's across the street. It's also home of the annual Spam Cookoff every May. There are some worn pool tables and video poker games if you're compelled to do something besides drink and chat up the locals who hang here. And if you really get bored, there's a dusty bookshelf filled with tattered paperbacks. It's the perfect place to nurse a hangover with a spicy Bloody Mary on Sundays.

Festivals

There are two major festivals in Vieques. The biggest one is **Fiestas Patronales de Nuestra Sra. Del Carmen** (787/741-5000), which is held on the plaza of Isabel Segunda Wednesday–Sunday during the third weekend of July. Attractions include parades, religious processions, a small carnival, and lots of live Latin music and dancing. Entertainment usually starts around 9 P.M. and lasts until the wee hours of the morning. Festivities are fueled by *bili*, a traditional beverage made from a local fruit called *quenepa* mixed with white rum, cinnamon, and sugar.

The other big event is the **Cultural Festival** (787/741-1717), sponsored by the Institute of Puerto Rican Culture at El Fortín Conde de Mirasol in Isabel Segunda after Easter. Festivities include folk music and dance performances, a craft fair, and a book fair.

SHOPPING

Shopping outlets are pretty limited in Vieques. For a quality selection of handmade crafts by local and other Caribbean artisans, there's **Kim's Cabin Clothing Boutique and Gifts** (136 Calle Flamboyan, Esperanza, 787/741-3145, daily 9:30 A.M.–5 P.M.). In addition to Haitian metal art and sea-glass earrings, you'll find tropical-print shirts and dresses imported from Indonesia.

Another good source for tropical-print clothing is **Luna Loca** (343 Carr. 200, Isabel Segunda, 787/741-0264, Mon.–Sat. 9 A.M.–5 P.M., Sun. 10 A.M.–4 P.M.). It also has a small selection of jewelry and framed photographs of the island by local artists.

Vibrant original paintings and prints on canvas of tropical flowers, fish, palm trees, and jungle scenes by local artist Siddhia Hutchinson can be found at **Siddhia Hutchinson Fine Art Design Studio and Gallery** (A-15 Calle Mon Repos, Isabel Segunda, 787/741-8780, siddhia@coqui.net, http://siddhiahutchinson.com, daily 9 A.M.–3 P.M.). The artwork has also been tastefully reproduced on ceramics, dinnerware, rugs, and pillows.

ACCOMMODATIONS
$50-100

If you don't mind not being on the beach, the best deal for the budget-minded traveler is **(Casa Alta Vista** (297 Calle Flamboyan, Esperanza, 787/741-3296, fax 787/741-3296, casaaltavista@yahoo.com, www.casaaltavista.net, $80 s, $90–95 d, $115–175 for 4 people, plus 9 percent tax). This small, cheerful 10-room guesthouse features newly renovated rooms with modern bathrooms and extra-comfy mattresses. There's no TV, telephone, or pool, but the air-conditioning and mini-refrigerator keep things cool. A rooftop sundeck offers a 360-degree view of the island, three-quarters of it ocean. If it's available, ask for room 12—it has got the best view of the ocean and hillsides. Registration is in the small market on the first floor. This is also where spontaneous jam sessions occasionally occur, thanks to owner and guitar player Mark Biron, who keeps maracas, sticks, cowbells, and *güiros* on hand for anybody who wants to join in. Scooter, bicycle, snorkeling gear, beach chair, umbrella, and cooler rentals are available on-site. There are also a one-bedroom apartment and wheelchair-accessible rooms.

Trade Winds Guest House and Restaurant (Calle Flamboyan, Esperanza, 787/741-8666, fax 787/741-2964, tradewns@coqui.net, www.enchanted-isle.com/tradewinds, $70 s, $80 d, plus 9 percent tax) is a better restaurant than it is a guesthouse, but it's conveniently situated in the middle of Esperanza and across the street from the *malécon* (sea walk). The 10 rooms are small, windowless, and Spartan, but they're clean and have firm mattresses. There's no TV or telephone, but some rooms have air-conditioning. The rooms open onto a scrappy courtyard with plastic patio furniture, and there's a decent restaurant and bar upstairs.

Just want a cheap place to crash? If you

don't plan to spend much time in your room, **Bananas Guesthouse** (Calle Flamboyan, Esperanza, 787/741-8700, atbananas@aol. com, www.bananasguesthouse.com, $55–85 s/d plus 9 percent tax) may meet your needs. In the back of the popular bar and restaurant, Bananas, this bare-bones guesthouse has eight small, rustic, dimly lit rooms with deck flooring. There's no TV or telephone, but some rooms have air-conditioning, screened porches, and mini-refrigerators.

Perched on an inland hillside overlooking the main island is the lovely, lushly landscaped ❦ **Crow's Nest Inn** (Carr. 201, km 1.1, Isabel Segunda, 787/741-0033 or 877/276-9763, fax 787/741-1294, thenest@coqui.net, www .crowsnestvieques.com, $90 s, $129 d, $139 one-bedroom suite, $250 two-bedroom suite, plus 9 percent tax; includes continental breakfast). The Spanish hacienda–style inn has 16 well-appointed modern rooms, all with air-conditioning, TV, and a kitchen or kitchenette. There are also a small pool and an excellent restaurant, Island Steakhouse. Snorkeling-gear rental is available.

There's something positively Mediterranean about the exterior appearance of **Casa La Lanchita** (374 N. Shore Rd., Isabel Segunda, 787/741-8449 or 800/774-4712, www .viequeslalanchita.com, $100–175, four-night minimum stay). The bright white four-story structure with archways and balustrades is built right on the sandy beach of a brilliant blue sea and is surrounded by flowering bougainvillea. Despite the posh exterior, the rooms are modestly appointed with budget rattan and metal furnishings, but each room has a private terrace and full-size kitchen.

$150-250

Luxury has many different definitions, and Vieques seems to have a unique hotel to match each one. The ultramodern boutique hotel ❦ **Bravo Beach Hotel** (1 N. Shore Rd., Isabel Segunda, 787/741-1128, info@bravobeachho-tel.com, www.bravobeachhotel.com, $160–215 s/d, $425 villa, plus 9 percent tax; no children under 18 permitted) is a study in glamorous minimalism. Nine rooms and a two-bedroom villa are located in a cluster of small bungalows painted pastel shades of green, blue, and yellow. Each room is different, but the spacious interiors all feature stark white walls that create a dramatic contrast to the dark mahogany platform beds and modular furnishings made of wood and glass. Some rooms have ocean-view balconies and floor-to-ceiling windows. One room has 180-degree windows and a king-size canopy bed. Each room has satellite TV, air-conditioning, a mini-refrigerator, wireless Internet, a DVD player, and a PlayStation. The bathroom is stocked with Aveda bath products, and the beds are made with Italian Frette linens. Although it's on the ocean, the hotel doesn't have a swimmable beach. Instead there are two swimming pools, one ocean-side. A poolside bar and lounge serves a limited menu, and the newly opened BBH restaurant serves tapas ranging $8–14 and boasts a large wine selection.

Victorian elegance is the theme at ❦ **Hacienda Tamarindo** (Calle Flamboyan, just west of Esperanza, 787/741-0420, fax 787/741-3215, hactam@aol.com, www.hacienda tamarindo.com, $125–230 s, $145–245 d, $175–230 suites, $200–270 two-bedroom suites, plus 9 percent tax and 10 percent service charge). Built around a 200-year-old tamarind tree that's rooted in the lobby and shades the second-floor breakfast room, this beautifully appointed hotel is furnished in a tasteful combination of antique Caribbean and Victorian styles. Folk art, wall murals, and vintage circus posters provide playful touches. There are 13 rooms and three suites. Each one is different, but they all contain basket-weave furnishings, brightly colored bedspreads, and air-conditioning. Rooms have neither TVs nor telephones, but each one comes with folding chairs, oversize towels, and coolers for the beach or pool. The hotel doesn't have a restaurant per se, but it does serve a free breakfast, and a box lunch can be prepared for $8.50 per person if requested the night before. There's also a 24-hour honor bar. No one under age 15 is permitted.

A romantic getaway doesn't get any more lovely or secluded than **Inn on the Blue**

Horizon (Calle Flamboyan, west of Esperanza, 787/741-3318 or 787/741-0527, fax 787/741-0522, innonblue@aol.com, www.innonthe bluehorizon.com, $160–370 s, plus 9 percent tax). The small 10-room inn perched on a cliff overlooking the ocean hosts many weddings and is geared primarily toward couples. Rooms are exquisitely furnished with poster beds, antiques, and original artwork. Amenities include a small gym, pool, lighted tennis courts, and an inviting pavilion bar. Rooms have air-conditioning, but no TV or telephone. **Carambola** restaurant serves upscale Caribbean fusion cuisine, and the **Blue Moon Bar and Grill** serves breakfast and lunch in a lovely open-air pavilion-style restaurant overlooking the ocean.

Avant-garde architecture in a thickly wooded setting distinguishes the most unusual hotel in Puerto Rico, **The Hix House** (Carr. 995, km 1.6, 787/741-2302 or 787/741-2797, info@hix-islandhouse.com, www.hixislandhouse.com, $195–325 d, plus 9 percent tax and 7 percent service charge). Four unpainted concrete buildings house 13 "lofts," many with open sides, outdoor showers, and ocean views. Designed by architect John Hix to have as little impact on its 13 acres as possible, the property uses solar energy and recycles used water to replenish the vegetation. There's no TV or telephone, but the linens are Frette, the pool is spectacular, and each morning the kitchen is stocked with juices, cereal, breads, and coffee. Yoga classes are conducted in the pavilion, and in-room or garden massages are available.

Over $250
Martineau Bay Resort and Spa (Carr. 200, km 3.4, Isabel Segunda, 787/741-4100, fax 787/741-4171) was closed for a massive remodel project in late 2008. An anomaly on Vieques, it's the first megaresort but most likely not the last. Formerly owned and operated by Wyndham and later bought by W Hotels, the complex has 156 rooms and villas, all either oceanfront or ocean-view. There are also one-to three-bedroom villas. Amenities include a large pool with swim-up bar, full-service spa, fitness room, beach access, tennis courts, and room service. All rooms have air-conditioning, satellite TV, CD players, coffeemakers, hair dryers, and private balconies or terraces. The rooms are large and ultraluxurious, featuring Spanish tile bathrooms, mahogany furniture, and amazing mattresses.

FOOD
Breakfast
There are several terrific breakfast spots in Vieques. In addition to your typical eggs, **Mamasonga** (Calle Plinio Peterson, Isabel Segunda, 787/741-0103, daily 8 A.M.–4 P.M., $3.95–8.95) serves great German apple pancakes and French toast, plus muesli for the health-conscious. Lunch items include black-bean soup, burgers, nachos, Cuban sandwiches, quesadillas, and salads. There's also a full bar.

Another option is **Belly Buttons Café and Grill** (62 Calle Flamboyan, Esperanza, 787/741-3336, daily 7:30 A.M.–2 P.M., $4.50–7.50), serving eggs, French toast, bagels, sandwiches, and salads outside on picnic tables. Call ahead for curb service.

Puerto Rican and Caribbean
Fine dining is a rarity in Vieques, so thank goodness for **❰ BBH** (Bravo Beach Hotel, 1 N. Shore Rd., Isabel Segunda, 787/741-1128, info@bravobeachhotel.com, www.bravobeach hotel.com, $6–14) with its creative, Caribbean-influenced menu of tapas. The menu is always changing, but plan to dine on the likes of house-cured olives, mussels, seared scallops, duck breast, or New Zealand lamb in the lovely serenity of the minimalist-style setting. Check out the outstanding wine selection in the walk-in wine gallery.

Because many restaurants on Vieques close early, it's good to know where to find a decent restaurant open later in the evening every day. That place is **Richard's Café Restaurant** (Carr. 200, just west of downtown Isabel Segunda, 787/741-5242, daily 11 A.M.–3 P.M. and 5–11 P.M., $6.95–18.95). The dim lighting, fast-food decor, and fake flowers don't create much of an atmosphere inside the pink concrete structure. But it serves good traditional

Puerto Rican cuisine, including *pastelillos, mofongo,* steak, seafood, and lobster. The full bar serves a terrific passion fruit punch, made with Grand Marnier, rum, and pineapple juice.

For a creative take on Caribbean cuisine, there's 🄲 **Restaurante Bilí** (Amapola Inn, 144 Calle Flamboyan, Esperanza, 787/741-1382, Wed.–Sun. 11 A.M.–4 P.M. and 6–11 P.M., $16.95–29.95). The casual, open-air restaurant's specialties include mini-*empanadillas* stuffed with rabbit and goat cheese, *dorado* in plantain chutney, whole fried snapper, and angel-hair pasta with crab meat stewed in coconut milk. There are also a full bar and a partial view of the ocean.

Also serving Caribbean cuisine is **Trade Winds Restaurant** (Calle Flamboyan, Esperanza, 787/741-8666, fax 787/741-2964, tradewns@coqui.net, www.enchanted-isle .com/tradewinds, daily 8:30 A.M.–2 P.M. and 6–9:30 P.M., $14.50–28). This casual open-air restaurant overlooks the water and serves grilled fish, steak, lobster, pork loin, pasta, *mofongo,* and coconut curry. For dessert, try the piña colada bread pudding with warm rum sauce. There are 10 small guest rooms behind the restaurant.

American and Fusion

Nearby is **Banana's Beach Bar and Grill** (Calle Flamboyan, Esperanza, 787/741-8700, daily 11 A.M.–about 10 P.M., bar stays open later, $5–16.50). This very casual, popular drinking hole serves mostly American pub fare, including burgers, wings, and hotdogs, as well as jerk chicken, ribs, and grilled fish. There are eight small guest rooms in the back.

Although its prices are fairly low by Vieques standards, the gorgeous ambience of 🄲 **Cafe Media Luna** (351 Antonio G. Mellado/Carr. 200, Isabel Segunda, 787/741-2594, Wed.–Sun. 7–10 P.M., $12–19) makes it feel like a special-occasion restaurant. Dark blue walls, terra-cotta tile floors, and Indian batik wall hangings set a sensual stage for its interesting combination of Asian and Mediterranean dishes, all made from scratch. Specialties include ginger shrimp pancakes with lemon-coconut sauce, avocado lime cucumber gazpacho, and parmigiana-rosemary–crusted rack of lamb.

Seafood and Steak

If you get your fill of seafood in Vieques, **Island Steakhouse** (Crow's Nest Guesthouse, Carr. 201, km 1.1, Isabel Segunda, 787/741-0033 or 877/276-9763, fax 787/741-1294, thenest@ coqui.net, www.crowsnestvieques.com, Fri.–Tues. 6–10 P.M., $8–27) is ready to serve your carnivorous needs: filet, sirloin, rib eye, porterhouse, *churrasco*—you name it, the place has got it. But non–meat-eaters aren't overlooked: The menu also features whole lobster, fried shrimp, and salmon.

Chez Shack (Carr. 995, km 1.8, 787/741-2175, Mon. and Wed.–Sat. 5:30–10 P.M., $12–30) really is a shack. It's constructed of tacked-up sheets of corrugated metal strung with twinkle lights and surrounded by thick forest, but folks flock here for good food and the steel-drum band. The kitchen has been undergoing some changes in its management and the type of cuisine it serves, and the hours seem to vary from week to week. But everyone swears by the excellent food and convivial mood of this bohemian eatery.

INFORMATION AND SERVICES

All of the services on Vieques are in Isabel Segunda. The **tourism office** (787/741-0800, Mon.–Fri. 9 A.M.–4 P.M.) is on the plaza in Casa Alcaldia (town hall). But for the most comprehensive, up-to-date information, visit www.enchanted-isle.com, www.vieques-island .com, www.viequestravelguide.com, and www .travelandsports.com/vie.htm.

To stay abreast of local news and events, pick up the island's two monthly publications, *Vieques Times* (153 Calle Flamboyan, Esperanza, www.viequestimes.com) and *Vieques Events* (www.viequesevents.net), both printed in English and Spanish.

The island's only bank, with an ATM, is **Banco Popular** (115 Calle Muñoz Rivera, 787/741-2071). Nearby, on the same street, is the **post office** (787/741-3891). You'll find the **police station** (787/741-2020 or 787/741-2121) at Carretera 200, km 0.2, at Carretera 997, and the **fire department** can be reached by calling 787/741-2111. For health services, **Centro de Salud de Familia** (Carr. 997) is open Monday–Friday 7 A.M.–3:30 P.M., and the emergency room is open 24 hours. Serving visitors' pharmacy needs is **Farmacia Antonio** (Calle Benitez Guzman across from Casa Alcaldia, 787/741-8397).

Self-serve laundry **Familia Ríos** (Calle Benítez Castaño, 787/438-1846) is open Sunday–Monday and Wednesday–Friday 6 A.M.–7 P.M., and Saturday 6 A.M.–5 P.M.

GETTING THERE
By Ferry
The **Puerto Rico Port Authority** (in Vieques 787/741-4761, 787/863-0705, or 800/981-2005, daily 8–11 A.M. and 1–3 P.M.) operates a daily ferry service between Vieques and Fajardo.

The **passenger ferry** is primarily a commuter operation, and it can often be crowded—especially on the weekends and holidays when vacationers swell the number of passengers. Reservations are not accepted, but you can buy tickets in advance. Arrive no later than one hour before departure. Sometimes the ferry cannot accommodate everyone who wants to ride. The trip typically takes about an hour to travel between Fajardo and Vieques, and the fare is $4 round-trip per person. Note that ferry schedules can change, but the schedule was as follows:

- **Fajardo to Vieques:** Monday–Friday 9:30 A.M., 1 P.M., 4:30 P.M., 8 P.M.; Saturday–Sunday and Monday holidays 9 A.M., 3 P.M., 6 P.M.

- **Vieques to Fajardo:** Monday–Friday 6:30 A.M., 11 A.M., 3 P.M., 6 P.M.; Saturday–Sunday and Monday holidays 6:30 A.M., 1 P.M., 4:30 P.M.

There is also a weekday **cargo/car ferry,** for which reservations are required. But be aware that most car-rental agencies in Puerto Rico do not permit their automobiles to leave the main island. The best option is to leave your car in

Fajardo and rent another car on Vieques. The trip usually takes about two hours, and the cost is $15 for small vehicles and $19 for large vehicles. The schedule is as follows:

- **Fajardo to Vieques:** Monday–Friday 4 A.M., 9:30 A.M., 4:30 P.M.

- **Vieques to Fajardo:** Monday 6 A.M., 1:30 P.M., 6 P.M.

By Air
As almost anyone who's taken the commuter ferry from Fajardo to Vieques will tell you, the best way to get to the island is by air. There are several small airlines that fly to Vieques from the main island, and the flights are fairly inexpensive and speedy.

In San Juan, flights can be arranged from Luis Muñoz Marín International Airport near Isla Verde or from the smaller Isla Grande Airport near Old San Juan. But the shortest, cheapest flight is from the newly opened Jose Aponte de la Torre Airport on the former Roosevelt Roads Naval Base in Ceiba on the east coast. Round-trip flights are about $190 from San Juan and $60 from Ceiba. Flights between Vieques and Culebra are about $70.

Service providers include **Isla Nena Air Service** (787/863-4447, 787/863-4449, or 877/812-5144, islanenapr@centennialpr.net, www.islanena.8m.com); **Vieques Air Link** (787/741-8331 or 888/901-9247, valair@coqui.net, www.viequesairlink.com); **M&N Aviation** (787/791-7008, www.mnaviation.com); and **Air Flamenco** (787/724-1818, airflamenco@hotmail.com, www.airflamenco.net).

GETTING AROUND
Unless you plan to park yourself at one of the island's few full-service hotels and never leave it, you're going to need a rental car to get around. *Publicos* are a great way to get from the ferry or airport to your hotel, but beyond that they're not as reliable as the taxi service mainland Americans may be accustomed to.

If you do rent a car, book it well in advance of your arrival. They get snapped up quickly.

Rental fees start around $50 per day, and penalties can be accrued if you return it with excessive sand inside, damp seats, or less gas in the tank than when you got it. Most vehicles are four-wheel drives because many of the beaches require off-roading to reach. Blowouts are not unusual, so make sure your car has a full-size replacement tire and the tools necessary to change it. If you need assistance changing the tire, the rental-car agency may send someone to help, but again, it will cost you. The seatbelt law is enforced, as are speed limits, which are mostly 35 miles per hour, except in town and on beach roads, where it's 10–15 miles per hour.

There are only three gas stations on the island, one of which appears to be perpetually closed. They're all within a short distance of one another on Carretera 200 in Isabel Segunda, just west of the plaza. Because gas is shipped from San Juan on weekdays only, gas shortages are not unusual, and sometimes gas stations close early on Sundays, since that's the day everyone goes to the beach, including the gas-station operators.

Remember that semiwild horses roam freely on Vieques. Because many roads in Vieques are unlit, it's nearly impossible to see the horses in the dark, so take extra care when driving at night.

Publico

Publicos can typically can be found waiting for fares at the airport or ferry. They can also be called randomly throughout the day for pickup service, although some travelers report that they are not always reliable or timely. Fares are typically $3 in town and $6 to various sites and beaches on the island.

The following is a partial list of *publicos* operating on the island: **Ana Robles or Rafael Perez** (787/313-0599 or 787/486-0267); **Eric** (787/741-0448); **Henry** (787/649-3838); and **Lolo Felix** (787/485-5447).

For travelers seeking transportation from San Juan to Fajardo to catch the ferry to Vieques, **Padin** operates 24-hour *publico* service between Fajardo and the Luis Muñoz Marín International Airport in San Juan. Call Mrs. Rivera at 787/644-3091 or 787/355-6746, or José Padin at 787/644-3091.

Car Rentals

Car rentals start at about $50 per day in Vieques, and most vehicles are jeeps or other four-wheel–drive automobiles. Some agencies will deliver a rental to the airport or your hotel; others require a *publico* ride to the office. Agencies include **Martineau Car Rental** (787/741-0087 or 787/741-3948, www.martineau carrental.com); **Vieques Car and Jeep Rental** (787/741-1037, viequescars@yahoo .com, www.viequescarrental.com); **Island Car Rental** (787/741-1666, iscar@coqui.net, www .enchanted-isle.com/islandcar/); and **Steve's Car Rental** (787/741-8135, stevescarrental@ aol.com, www.enchanted-isle.com/steves). Scooter rentals are available at **Extreme Scooters** (Calle Flamboyan, Esperanza, 787/435-9345).

VIEQUES AND CULEBRA

Culebra

As laid-back as Vieques is, it's practically Las Vegas compared to Culebra. Halfway between mainland Puerto Rico and St. Thomas, the tiny amoeba-shaped archipelago with 23 surrounding cays is just four miles by seven miles. The island is home to 3,000 residents and has one small community—**Dewey** (commonly called "Pueblo" or "Town")—on Ensenada Honda harbor, where the ferry docks.

Culebra has yet to be discovered by the tourism industry, but experienced divers know it as one of the best diving spots in the Caribbean. The clear clean waters are practically untouched by people and their polluting by-products, thanks in part to the arid island's absence of rivers or streams. The result is superb underwater visibility and healthy, intact coral systems that support a wide variety of sea life.

Recognizing the island's vital role as a natural wildlife habitat, President Theodore Roosevelt proclaimed much of the island a National Wildlife Refuge in 1909, which today encompasses 1,568 acres. Nonetheless, in 1939 the U.S. Navy made Culebra its primary gunnery and bomb practice site and continued its operations here until 1975, when it turned its focus to Vieques.

The island is a combination of hilly terrain with dry subtropical forest and a highly irregular coastline punctuated by cliffs, mangrove forests, and spectacular sandy coral beaches. Because it is so sparsely inhabited, Culebra is home to many endangered species and is an important nesting site for birds and sea turtles. Playa Flamenco is celebrated as one of the best beaches in the United States. But there are many other smaller beaches to discover, some completely deserted much of the time.

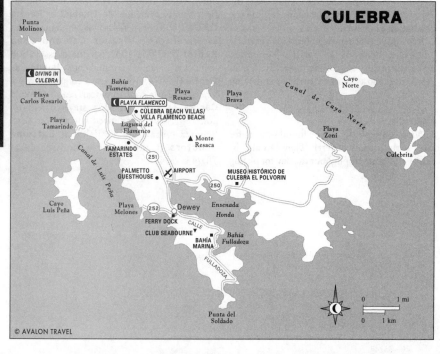

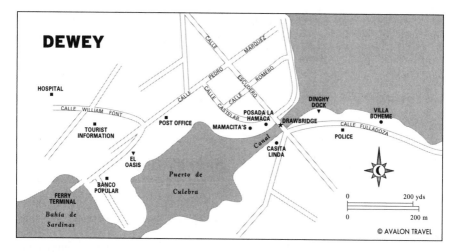

DEWEY

HOSPITAL

CALLE WILLIAM FONT

TOURIST INFORMATION

POST OFFICE

POSADA LA HAMACA

MAMACITA'S

DRAWBRIDGE

DINGHY DOCK

VILLA BOHEME

CALLE FULLADOZA

POLICE

CASITA LINDA

Canal

EL OASIS

BANCO POPULAR

FERRY TERMINAL

Puerto de Culebra

Bahía de Sardinas

CALLE MARQUEZ

CALLE PEDRO

CALLE ESCUDERO

CALLE ROMERO

CALLE CASTELAR

0   200 yds

0   200 m

© AVALON TRAVEL

Accommodations in Culebra are mostly small mom-and-pop guesthouses, some little more than spare bedrooms. The operations here are mostly self-serve. In fact, it's not unusual for visitors to have the run of the place when owners decide to head to the beach or bar to while away the day. But there are a handful of small luxury hotels and condo rental units for travelers who want more modern-day amenities or services. There are a dozen or so restaurants, where service typically moves at a snail's pace, and a couple of bars, but little real nightlife.

Because water is shipped from San Juan, shortages are not unusual, and pressure is often low. Some smaller properties have limited hot water or none at all. Plumbing in general can be problematic—the standard practice is to discard toilet paper in the trash instead of flushing it. And alarm clocks are never necessary, because you're sure to be woken by one of the roosters that roam the island. An anomaly in the world, Culebra is virtually crime-free. Instead of petty theft, visitors need only brace themselves against the voracious mosquitoes and sand gnats that tend to invade around dusk.

Culebra is one of the last vestiges of pre-tourism Puerto Rico. Nobody's in a hurry, modern conveniences are few, and all anybody really wants to do is go to the beach. That's the way

people in Culebra like it, and most of them want to keep it that way. Visitors are advised to embrace the island's quirky inconveniences and sleepy pace of life to fully appreciate its many rare charms.

SIGHTS

If you spend any time in Culebra, you're bound to enter the **Culebra National Wildlife Refuge** (787/742-0115, Mon.–Fri. 7:30 A.M.–4 P.M.). It encompasses 1,568 acres, including much of Flamenco Peninsula, where 60,000 sooty terns nest, as well as mangrove forests, wetlands, coastline, surrounding cays (except Cayo Norte), and **Monte Resaca,** the island's highest point at 650 feet, which contains forested canyons, ravines, and a unique habitat known as the boulder forest. The refuge contains excellent beaches, diving, bird-watching, and hiking. Culebrita, Cayo Luis Peña, and Monte Resaca are open daily sunrise–sunset. Other areas are off-limits to visitors. For maps and information, visit the refuge office, east on Carretera 250, just past the cemetery.

Museo Histórica de Culebra El Polvorin (off Carr. 250 toward Playa Brava, 787/405-3768 or 787/742-3832, Thurs.–Sun. 10 A.M.–3 P.M.) is a newly created museum of history on the island that features old maps and photographs of Culebra, Taíno artifacts, traditional canoes made from the zinc plant, and Navy artifacts. It's located at the site of the first settlement in Culebra, in a 1905-era stone building that once stored ammunitions for the Navy.

BEACHES

Once you see Culebra's craggy coastline of hidden coves, private beaches, coral outcroppings, and cays, it's easy to imagine why pirates liked to hide out here. Playa Flamenco is the island's most celebrated beach, and rightly so. But there are many less populated and more remote beaches to be found for those willing to hike in.

◖ Playa Flamenco

Named one of "America's Best Beaches" by the Travel Channel, Playa Flamenco (north on Carr. 251 at dead-end) is one of the main reasons people come to Culebra. It's a wide, mile-long, horseshoe-shaped beach with calm, shallow waters and fine white sand. The island's only publicly maintained beach, it has

bathroom facilities, picnic tables, lounge-chair and umbrella rentals, and a camping area. You can buy sandwiches and alcoholic beverages at Coconuts Beach Grill in front of Culebra Beach Villa, as well as from vendors who set up grills and blenders in the ample parking lot. An abandoned, graffiti-covered tank remains as a reminder of the Navy's presence. It can get crowded on summer weekends and holidays—especially Easter and Christmas.

Other Beaches

If Playa Flamenco is too crowded, take a 20-minute hike over the ridge and bypass the first small beach you encounter to reach the more private **Playa Carlos Rosario,** a pleasant, narrow beach flanked by coral reef and boulders. It offers excellent snorkeling around the long, vibrant stretch of coral reef not too far offshore. Other great snorkeling and diving beaches are **Punta Soldado** (south of Dewey, at the end of Calle Fulladoza), which also has beautiful coral reefs; **Playa Melones,** a rocky beach and subtropical forest within walking

Playa Carlos Rosario has an excellent reef for snorkeling and diving.

© JIM JOHNSON

VIEQUES AND CULEBRA

distance of Dewey; and **Playa Tamarindo,** where you'll find a diversity of soft corals and sea anemones.

Excellent deserted beaches can also be found on two of Culebra's cays—**Cayo Luis Peña** and **Culebrita,** which is distinguished by a lovely but crumbling abandoned lighthouse and several tidal pools. To gain access, it is necessary to either rent a boat or arrange a water taxi. And be sure to bring water, sunscreen, and other provisions; there are no facilities or services on the islands.

At the far eastern side of the island at the end of Carretera 250 is **Playa Zoni,** which features a frequently deserted sandy beach and great views of Culebrita, Cayo Norte, and St. Thomas.

Playa Brava has the biggest surf on the island, but it requires a bit of a hike to get there. To reach the trailhead, travel east on Carretera 250 and turn left after the cemetery, and then hike downhill and fork to the left. Note that Playa Brava is a turtle-nesting site, so it may be off-limits during nesting season from April to June.

Like Playa Brava, **Playa Resaca** is an important nesting site for sea turtles, but it is ill-suited for swimming because of the coral reef along the beach. The hike to Playa Resaca is fairly arduous, but it traverses a fascinating topography through a mangrove and boulder forest. To get there, turn on the road just east of the airport off Carretera 250, drive to the end, and hike the rest of the way in.

Turtle Watch

Culebra is one of three nesting grounds for hawksbill and leatherback turtles, the latter of which is the largest species of turtle in the world, weighing between 500 and 1,600 pounds. From April to early June, the sea turtles spend the evenings trudging up the beach at Playa Resaca and Playa Brava to dig holes and lay eggs before returning to the sea in grand displays of sand-tossing to cover their tracks. The Puerto Rico Department of Natural and

© JIM JOHNSON

Visitors must take precautions not to disturb the sea turtles during nesting season, from April to June.

VIEQUES AND CULEBRA

Environmental Resources (787/556-6234 or 877/77-CORAL—877/772-6725, fax 530/618-4605, info@coralations.org, www .coralations.org/turtles) accepts volunteers to catalog the turtles when they nest.

SPORTS AND RECREATION

C Diving

Culebra more than makes up for its dearth of entertainment options with its wealth of diving opportunities. There are reportedly 50 dive sites surrounding the island. They're mostly along the island's fringe reefs and around the cays. In addition to huge diverse coral formations, divers commonly spot sea turtles, stingrays, puffer fish, angel fish, nurse sharks, and more.

Among the most popular dive sites are **Carlos Rosario (Impact),** which features a long, healthy coral reef teeming with sea life, including huge sea fans, and **Shipwreck,** the site of *The Wit Power,* a tugboat sunk in 1984. Here you can play out your *Titanic* fantasies and witness how the sea has claimed the boat for its habitat.

Many of the best dive sites are around Culebra's many cays. **Cayo Agua Rock** is a single 45-foot-tall rock surrounded by sand and has been known to attract barracudas, nurse sharks, and sea turtles. **Cayo Ballena** provides a 120-foot wall dive with spectacular coral. **Cayo Raton** is said to attract an inordinate number and variety of fish. And **Cayo Yerba** features an underwater arch covered in yellow cup coral, best seen at night when they "bloom," and a good chance to see stingrays.

The island's sole diving and snorkeling source, **Culebra Divers** (across from the ferry terminal in Dewey, 787/742-0803, info@culebradivers.com, www.culebradivers.com), offers daily snorkeling trips for $45. One-tank dives are $60, and two-tank dives are $85, including tanks and weights. Snorkeling and dive gear is available for rent. It's also a good place to go for advice on snorkeling from the beach.

Other Water Sports

For water-sport equipment rentals, **Culebra**

Water Toys (next to El Batey in Dewey, 787/742-1122, cell 787/246-1718 or 787/406-2224, www.islaculebra.com/culebra-water-toys/english.html, daily 8 A.M.–5 P.M.) offers snorkel gear for $10, kayaks and pedal boats for $40, rowboats for $50, sailboard gear for $60, and fishing skiffs for $125. It also offers water-taxi service to Culebrita, Cayo Luis Peña, Carlos Rosario, Vieques, and St. Thomas.

Mountain Biking

Culebra Bike Shop (Calle Fulladoza, 787/742-2209 or 787/209-2543, daily 9 A.M.–6 P.M.) rents 21- and 24-speed mountain bikes, as well as boogie boards and snorkeling equipment.

ENTERTAINMENT

Nightlife is limited on Culebra, but sometimes even nature lovers and beachcombers need to cut loose. **El Batey** (Carr. 250, km 1.1, 787/742-3828, Fri.–Sat. 10 P.M.–2 A.M., also serves lunch) provides that opportunity. Dancing is the primary attraction at this large no-frills establishment, where DJs spin salsa, merengue, and disco on Friday and Saturday nights. It also serves deli sandwiches and burgers ($3–5) during the day.

Everybody who goes to Culebra ends up at **Mamacita's** (64 Calle Castelar, 787/742-0090, www.mamacitaspr.com, Sun.–Thurs. 4–10 P.M., Fri.–Sat. 4–11 P.M.) at some point. The popular open-air watering hole right on the canal in Dewey attracts both locals and visitors alike. Two side-by-side tin-roofed pavilions provide shade for the cozy oasis appointed with brightly painted tables and chairs surrounded by potted palms. The blue tiled bar is tricked out with colorful folk art touches painted in shades of turquoise, lime green, and lavender. Behind the bar you can buy cigarettes and condoms, and you can get a spritz of bug spray free of charge when the sand gnats attack. Happy hour is 3–6 P.M. daily. Try the house special cocktail, the bushwhacker, a frozen concoction of Kahlúa, Bailey's Irish Cream, coconut cream, rum, and amaretto. Check the chalkboard for excellent daily dinner specials.

SHOPPING

Shopping is limited to mostly shops selling tourist trinkets, but **Butiki** (74 Calle Romero, Dewey, daily 9 A.M.–6 P.M., 708/935-2542, www.butikiculebra.com) stands out for offering a great selection of batik fabrics, purses, jewelry by local artisans, and seascape oil paintings by owner Evan Schwarze.

ACCOMMODATIONS

Some properties require a minimum stay, although exceptions may be made for a surcharge. It's worth asking if you don't mind the extra cost.

Under $50

Playa Flamenco Campground (Playa Flamenco, 787/742-7000, $20, cash only) is not necessarily the place to go if you want a quiet spot to commune with nature. It's more like party central on weekends, holidays, and in summer, when the grounds can get crowded. Facilities include toilets, outdoor showers, and picnic tables. Reservations are required. If you can't get through by phone, write Autoridad de Conservación y Dessarrollo de Culebra, Attn.: Playa Flamenco, Apartado 217, Culebra, PR 00775.

$50-100

The majority of Culebra's properties are small, modest self-serve operations that are more true to the rustic spirit of the island. Staying at **Villa Arynar B&B** (Calle Fulladoza on Ensenada Honda bay, 787/742-3145, berniefrancette@ cs.com, www.culebra-island.com, Oct.–May, $90 s/d, $595 week) is like visiting friends. The two-story private home is right on the bay and surrounded by vegetation. Accommodations are limited to two spare bedrooms with a shared bathroom, but guests are free to enjoy the large decks, fishing pier, and common room with couches and a refrigerator. Owners and visitors alike eat breakfast together on the deck. Adults only.

For those who want to stay in the town of Dewey, just walking distance from the ferry dock, there are several options. **Mamacita's**

Guesthouse (64 Calle Castelar, 787/742-0090, $102. s, $115 d, including tax) is a pastel-colored hodgepodge of balconies and archways squeezed between Calle Castelar and the canal. The hostel-like accommodations are strictly functional and feature air-conditioning and satellite TV in the bedrooms. It's best suited for those just looking for a place to crash and a hopping bar and excellent restaurant on-site. Laundry facilities and boat dockage are available for guests. Internet access is available for a fee.

Visitors get more bang for the buck next door at **Posada La Hamaca** (68 Calle Castelar, 787/742-3516, info@posada.com, www.posada.com, $85 s, $97 d, $108 studio, $160 one-bedroom that sleeps 8, plus 9 percent tax). The Spanish-style guesthouse is under new management and has updated itself with new furnishings and fresh paint inside and out. The 10 rooms are light, airy and tidy, and they come with satellite TV, air-conditioning, mini-refrigerators, free Internet, and hot water. There's a large shady deck overlooking the canal out back with two gas grills. Beach towels, coolers, and free ice are provided for trips to the beach.

Palmetto Guesthouse (128 Manuel Vasquez, two blocks behind Carlos Jeep, 787/742-0257 or 787/235-6736, palmettoculebra@yahoo.com, www.palmettoculebra.com, $96 s, $115 d) is a modest six-unit property in the residential part of Dewey, within walking distance of the airport. One of the few properties that doesn't boast a view of the water, it makes up for its location with the "we aim to please" attitude of its owners, former Peace Corps volunteers Mark and Terrie Hayward. The small, tidy rooms are appointed with modern furnishings, air-conditioning, and mini-refrigerators. Common areas include two kitchens, a computer with Internet access, and a TV with a DVD/VCR player (but no cable or satellite access). Beach chairs, umbrellas, boogie boards, and coolers are provided free of charge for a small deposit. The shady backyard has a deck and gas grill. Co-owner Mark Hayward also operates an informational website on Culebra at http://culebrablog.com.

$100-150

Despite its weathered exterior, **Casita Linda** (by canal bridge in Dewey, 787/435-0430 or 787/742-0360, casitalindabeach@cs.com, $119–225) offers three simple, cheerful, modern one- and two-bedroom apartments on the canal. Amenities include kitchens or kitchenettes, air-conditioning in the bedrooms, and porches, patios, or terraces. Some units sleep up to six people.

Villa Boheme (368 Calle Fulladoza, 787/742-3508, http://villaboheme.com, $95–125 s, $130–135 d, plus 9 percent tax) has a lovely Spanish hacienda–style exterior and landscaped grounds right on Fulladoza Bay. Inside are 11 cheerfully appointed rooms with air-conditioning and hot water. Some rooms have private balconies and small kitchens; others share a communal kitchen in the patio area, which also contains satellite TV. A large terrace spans the length of the rambling property and overlooks the bay. Guests may use the dock, equipped with water and electricity, for $2 per foot per night. Moorings are also available for rent.

In town on Ensenada Honda is **Casa Ensenada** (142 Calle Escudero, 787/742-3559 or 866/210-00709, www.casaensenada.com, $125–175 for two, plus 9 percent tax). Despite its small size and modest aesthetics, this three-room guesthouse has everything you could need. Rooms are outfitted with air-conditioning, satellite TV, VCRs, hot showers, and kitchenettes, and there are a telephone, high-speed Internet, fax, and copier on-site. For trips to the beach, towels, chairs, coolers, umbrellas, and ice are available.

Nearby is **Vista Bella Apartments** (on Ensenada Honda, 787/644-6300 or 787/742-0549, visabellaculebra@yahoo.com, www.culebra-island.com, $120 studio, $163 one-bedroom that sleeps four, $218 two-bedroom that sleeps six). Four new, modern, and spacious apartments come with kitchens, air-conditioning, large covered balconies, and a spectacular view of Ensenada Honda.

$150-250

There are two hotels right on Playa Flamenco, which is the main reason to recommend either one. Just be sure to bring your insect repellent—it gets buggy. **Culebra Beach Villas** (Playa Flamenco, 787/767-7575, 787/754-6236, or 877/767-7575, cbrental@prtc.net, www.culebrabeachrental.com, $125 studio, $175–185 one-bedroom, $225 two-bedroom, plus 9 percent tax) offers 33 individually owned cottages and rooms with air-conditioning and kitchens, some with TVs but no Internet or telephones. The rooms are fairly Spartan, but the cottages have decks and covered porches. The service is minimal, although linens and towels are provided. Request a newer unit in the back of the complex if available. Basic pub fare can be had at the open-air waterside Coconuts Beach Grill.

The other option is **Villa Flamenco Beach** (Playa Flamenco, 787/742-0023, Nov.–Aug., $140 efficiency, $120–135 studio, plus 9 percent tax). A party-hardy vibe emanates from the two-story pink-and-green concrete structure, which contains six units. There are four studio apartments with kitchenettes, air-conditioning, and hot water, which sleep two, and two efficiency apartments with full kitchens, hot water in the shower only, and no air-conditioning, which sleep four. A couple of rooms have beachfront balconies. The place is low-key and self-serve.

The most luxurious option in this price range is **Club Seabourne** (Carr. 252, Calle Fulladoza on Ensenada Honda, 787/742-3169 or 800/981-4435, fax 787/742-0210, www.clubseabourne.com, $189 pool cabana room, $219 one-bedroom villa, $329 two-bedroom, including tax), which qualifies as Culebra's first foray into the world of modern boutique hotels. The quiet, remote, 14-unit hotel features a cluster of old-fashioned yellow-clapboard free-standing villas with pitched tin roofs that overlook Fulladoza Bay on Ensenada Honda. Rooms have air conditioning, but no TV or telephones. A lovely landscaped pool surrounded by umbrella tables overlooks the bay, as does the poolside bar, Sea Shells Bar and Grill. Fine dining can be had at White Sands Restaurant, serving Caribbean cuisine on a screened porch. Rates include continental breakfast, courtesy cocktails, one hour of free kayak rental, and transportation to and from the airport and ferry. Kayaks, snorkeling equipment, bikes, beach chairs, and umbrellas are available for rental, and picnic lunches are available by request.

Even more modern amenities can also be found at **Bahía Marina** (Punta Soldado Rd., km 2.4, 787/742-0535, 866/CULEBRA—866/285-3272, fax 787/742-0536, info@bahia-marina.net, www.bahiamarina.net, $151–179 one-bedroom apartment, $295 two-bedroom, plus tax). This hilltop row of 16 corporate-looking apartments with sleeper sofas in the sitting rooms comes with kitchenettes, air-conditioning, cable TV, and ocean-view balconies. There's also a large pool and an open-air bar and restaurant.

For total seclusion, you can't do much better than **Tamarindo Estates** (off Carr. 251 just south of Playa Flamenco, 787/742-3343, jose2@tamarindoestates.com, www.tamarindo estates.com, $190 plus $20 per pair of children, plus 9 percent tax). The property is on the wildlife refuge and features 12 simply furnished, hillside cottages on 60 acres overlooking the water and Cayo Luis Peña. Units are three or six to a building, and they look like they were furnished by a flea market, which gives them a quaint homespun vibe. Each one contains a TV, a VCR, air-conditioning in the bedroom, a fully equipped kitchen, a screened porch, and a rooftop veranda. Internet access is available in the common computer room. The rocky beach directly in front of the property offers great snorkeling, and a short hike north is a sandy beach for swimming. There's also a small pool on-site, but no restaurant or bar.

FOOD

Culebra is not particularly renowned for its restaurants, although there are a couple of establishments that are changing that. The concept of service is very different here from what stateside dwellers may be accustomed to. Things move at a slow, casual pace, so it's best to be patient and prepared to linger for awhile. Also,

note that operating hours can change unexpectedly, and some restaurants close up shop completely for weeks at a time.

Puerto Rican

Most of the restaurants in Culebra serve fairly modest fare. One popular spot is **Dinghy Dock** (Calle Fulladoza, south of the drawbridge, on Ensenada Honda, 787/742-0024, 787/742-0233, or 787/742-0518, info@dinghydock. com, www.dinghydock.com, daily 8 A.M.–2:30 P.M., 6:30–9 P.M., dinner $9–30). The name of this funky little eatery and bar is self-explanatory: Boats literally dock beside your table at this casual waterfront spot. Plastic patio chairs line a narrow dock under a hanging roof. The cuisine is by and large Puerto Rican, featuring Angus steaks and seafood, including tuna and lobster at night, waffles and French toast for breakfast. Check out the huge tarpon that swim below waiting for a handout. There is a full bar.

Seafood and Steak

The sensual delights of ◖ **Juanita Bananas** (1 Barrio Melones, 787/742-3171 or 787/402-5852, www.juanitabananas.com, Fri.–Mon. 5:30–10 P.M., $22–32, cash only) start before you even enter this romantic yet casual fine-dining restaurant. The Eden-like grounds are filled with flowers, fruit trees, fresh herbs, and a vegetable garden, which provide many of the ingredients in chef Jennifer Daubon's sublime contemporary Caribbean cuisine. Specialties include *panko*-crusted snapper, citrus-marinated salmon, and conch fritters. Sundays feature sushi specials. Reservations suggested, and BYOB.

Another romantic fine-dining option is Club Seabourne resort's **White Sands Restaurant** (Calle Fulladoza on Ensenada Honda, 787/742-3169, fax 787/742-0210, www.clubseabourne .com, Wed.–Sun. 6–9:30 P.M., $18–22). A cozy screened porch overlooking Fulladoza Bay is the setting for a menu with an emphasis on seafood, including lobster, scallops, salmon, and halibut.

Dining doesn't get much more casual than

at **Barbara Rosa** (189 Calle Escudero, 787/397-1923, Tues.–Sun. 11:30 A.M.–9 P.M., $6–16, cash only) where you literally dine in the front yard of the cook's house. Diners peruse a handwritten menu and place their orders at the counter for excellent, inexpensive seafood dishes, including fish and chips, crab cakes, and *dorado*.

Mamacita's (64 Calle Castelar, by the canal south of the drawbridge, 787/742-0322, restaurant daily 8 A.M.–3 P.M. and 6–9 P.M., bar Sun.–Thurs. 10 A.M.–10 P.M., Fri. 10 A.M.–11 P.M., $14–20, plus 15 percent gratuity) is a colorful open-air restaurant and bar serving excellent Caribbean-American–style dishes featuring *dorado, churrasco,* pork, and pasta, as well as a few pub-style appetizers. The dinner menu changes nightly and recently included a terrific dish of grilled *dorado* in cilantro lime aioli. Mamacita's doubles as a popular watering hole at night and rents rooms too.

Shipwreck Bar and Grill (at Bahía Marina, Calle Punta Soldado, km 2.4, 787/742-0535, www.bahiamarina.net, daily 4–10 P.M., $10–24) is a casual open-air eatery in the corporate environs of the Bahía Marina hotel, high up on a hill overlooking the water. The menu serves everything from burgers and conch fritters to whole snapper, *mofongo,* and New York strips.

Italian

El Eden & Neptune Bar (on an unnamed gravel road across the canal from Mamacita's, Dewey, 787/742-0509, Thurs.–Sat. 9 A.M.–9 P.M., Sun. 9 A.M.–2 P.M., Mon. 9 A.M.–6 P.M., $17–24) is a quirky little place owned by Richard Cantwell and Luz Rivera, who have put a lot of love and care into this eclectic combination deli, fine dining restaurant, tiki bar, wine shop, and grocery. All breads and desserts are made on-site using minimal processed foods and as many local products as possible. Lunch features deli sandwiches and daily specials, and the dinner menu changes weekly, but the risottos are their specialty. Other options may include gnocchi in pesto, veal marsala, and *churrasco*. For dessert,

try the passion fruit or Kahlúa mousse. There's a great tiki bar with shell-encrusted mirrors and bamboo if you just want to drink.

Lunch and Light Fare

Pandeli Bakery (17 Calle Pedro Marquez at the corner of Calle Escudero, Carr. 250, 787/742-0296, Mon.–Sat. 5:30 A.M.–5 P.M., Sun. 6:30 A.M.–5 P.M., $2.25–5.95) is a cool, modern, cozy bakery serving breakfast, sandwiches, burgers, empanadas, and pastries. There's also a small selection of dry goods and wines.

Hot pizza and ice-cold beer are the reasons to visit **El Oasis** (Calle Pedro Marquez, Dewey, 787/742-3175, Thurs.–Mon. 6–10 P.M., $7–20, cash only). The menu includes a few pasta dishes and salads, and the bar is a popular gathering spot for the drinking crowd.

Visitors to Playa Flamenco can find sustenance at **Coconuts Beach Grill** (in front of Culebra Beach Villas, $3–6, cash only). Its hours are irregular, but usually on the weekends this casual open-air eatery serves a limited selection of sandwiches and cocktails.

INFORMATION AND SERVICES

The **Culebra Tourism Department** (787/742-3521 or 787/742-3116, ext. 441 or 442, Mon.–Fri. 8 A.M.–4:30 P.M.) is in the yellow concrete building on Calle William Font in Dewey. For the most up-to-date information on the island, visit www.culebra-island.com, www.islaculebra.com, and www.culebra.org.

Because many businesses accept only cash, it's important to know where the island's ATM is. **Banco Popular** (787/742-3572, Mon.–Fri. 8:30 A.M.–3:30 P.M.) is across from the ferry terminal on Calle Pedro Marquez. You'll find the **post office** (787/742-3862, Mon.–Fri. 8 A.M.–4:30 P.M.) at 26 Calle Pedro Marquez, and **laundry facilities** can be found at Mamacita's Guesthouse (64 Calle Castelar, 787/742-0090).

The **police department** (787/742-3501) is on Calle Fulladoza just past Dinghy Dock. For medical services, **Hospital de Culebra** (Calle

William Font, 787/742-3511 or 787/742-0001, ambulance 787/742-0208) operates a clinic Monday–Friday 7 A.M.–4:30 P.M., as well as 24-hour emergency service and the island's only pharmacy.

GETTING THERE
By Ferry

The **Puerto Rico Port Authority** (in Culebra 787/742-3161, 787/741-4761, 787/863-0705, or 800/981-2005) operates a daily ferry service between Culebra and Fajardo from the town of Dewey.

The **passenger ferry** is primarily a commuter operation, and it can often be crowded—especially on the weekends and holidays. Reservations are not accepted, but you can buy tickets in advance. Be aware that on weekends and holidays, the ferry can sell out, leaving disappointed travelers behind. The trip typically takes about 1.5 hours to travel between Fajardo and Culebra. The fare is $4.50 round-trip per person, with an additional charge of $2 for beach or camping equipment. Note that ferry schedules can change, but the schedule was as follows:

- **Fajardo to Culebra:** Daily 9 A.M., 3 P.M., 7 P.M.

- **Culebra to Fajardo:** Daily 6:30 A.M., 1 P.M., 5 P.M.

There is also a weekday **cargo/car ferry** between Culebra and Fajardo, for which reservations are required. But be aware that most car-rental agencies in Puerto Rico do not permit their automobiles to leave the main island. The best option is to leave your car in Fajardo and rent another car on Culebra. The trip usually takes about 2.5 hours, and the cost is $15 for small vehicles and $19 for large vehicles. The schedule is as follows:

- **Fajardo to Culebra:** Monday, Tuesday, and Thursday 4 A.M. and 4:30 P.M.; Wednesday and Friday 4 A.M., 9:30 A.M., 4:30 P.M.

- **Culebra to Fajardo:** Monday, Tuesday, and Thursday 7 A.M. and 6 P.M.; Wednesday and Friday 7 A.M., 1 P.M., 6 P.M.

By Air

There are several small airlines that fly to Culebra from the main island, and the flights are fairly inexpensive and speedy. The only catch is that it's not for the faint of heart. Landing on the tiny island requires a steep descent over a mountaintop that takes your breath away.

In San Juan, flights can be arranged from Isla Grande Airport for about $190 round-trip, or from the new Jose Aponte de la Torre Airport in Ceiba, on the east coast of the big island, for about $66 round-trip. Service providers include **Isla Nena Air Service** (787/863-4447, 787/863-4449, or 877/812-5144, islanenapr@centennialpr.net, www.islanena.8m.com); **Vieques Air Link** (787/741-8331 or 888/901-9247, valair@coqui.net, www.viequesairlink.com); **M&N Aviation** (787/791-7008, www.mnaviation.com); and **Air Flamenco** (787/724-1818, airflamenco@hotmail.com, www.airflamenco.net).

Isla Nena Air Service also provides service between Culebra and Vieques for about $70.

GETTING AROUND

Between the *publicos* and water taxis, it is possible to get around Culebra without renting a vehicle, but it is not necessarily advisable. If you want to explore the island, jeeps and scooters are available for rent. Just be sure to book early—two to three months in advance is recommended.

There are few roads on Culebra, but they can be narrow, steep, and riddled with potholes. Parking and seatbelt laws are strictly enforced, and for some odd reason, driving bare-chested can get you a ticket.

Note that many places don't have traditional addresses with street names and numbers. If you ask people for an address, they're more likely to describe its physical location in relation to something else, as in "beside El Batey," or "across from the ferry." Also, nobody who lives in Culebra calls Dewey by its name. It's usually just referred to as "Pueblo" or "Town."

Water Taxi

There are several water-taxi operators who will take you to Culebrita for about $40 and to Cayo Luis Peña for $25. They include **Culebra Dive Shop** (787/742-0566); **Willy's Water Taxi** (787/742-3537); and **Culebra Water Toys** (787/742-1122, cell 787/246-1718 or 787/406-2224), which also provides service to Carlos Rosario, Vieques, and St. Thomas.

Cayo Norte Water Taxi (787/742-0169 or 646/924-6362) provides service to Cayo Norte.

Publico

If you arrive at the airport and there aren't any *publicos* there, strike out walking a short distance to Willys. From the airport turn left and go one block past the stop sign; he's on the right. Otherwise, you can give one a call to take you from point A to point B, although night service can be spotty. Operators include **Willys** (787/742-3537), **Kiko** (787/514-0453), **Samuel** (787/649-9641), and **Seguramente** (787/590-1375). It costs $2 to go from the airport to "downtown" Dewey or from Dewey to Flamenco Bay.

Car Rentals

Several agencies provide jeep rentals for about $60 per day, although some travelers report success at negotiating a better rate. Bring a copy of your insurance policy to avoid steep insurance charges. The following operators provide delivery service at the airport, ferry, or hotel of choice: **Jerry's Jeeps** (across from the Culebra airport entrance, 787/742-0587 or 787/742-0526); **Carlos Jeep Rental** (787/742-3514 or 787/613-7049, cjrental@coqui.net); and **Dick and Cathie's Jeep Rental** (787/742-0062, cash only).

Another option is to rent a scooter from **Culebra Scooter Rental** (at the Culebra airport, 787/742-0195, www.culebrascooterrental.com, 8:30 A.M.–6 P.M., $40 per day).

www.moon.com

DESTINATIONS | ACTIVITIES | BLOGS | MAPS | BOOKS

MOON.COM is ready to help plan your next trip! Filled with fresh trip ideas and strategies, author interviews, informative travel blogs, a detailed map library, and descriptions of all the Moon guidebooks, Moon.com is all you need to get out and explore the world—or even places in your own backyard. While at Moon.com, sign up for our monthly e-newsletter for updates on new releases, travel tips, and expert advice from our on-the-go Moon authors. As always, when you travel with Moon, expect an experience that is uncommon and truly unique.

MOON IS ON FACEBOOK—BECOME A FAN!
JOIN THE MOON PHOTO GROUP ON FLICKR

MAP SYMBOLS

▦ Expressway	**◖** Highlight	✕ Airfield	⚲ Golf Course
Primary Road	○ City/Town	✈ Airport	**P** Parking Area
Secondary Road	◉ State Capital	▲ Mountain	▱ Archaeological Site
Unpaved Road	⊛ National Capital	✛ Unique Natural Feature	♦ Church
Trail	★ Point of Interest		⛽ Gas Station
Ferry	● Accommodation	⟿ Waterfall	Glacier
Railroad	▼ Restaurant/Bar	♠ Park	Mangrove
Pedestrian Walkway	■ Other Location	⯃ Trailhead	Reef
Stairs	Λ Campground	⛷ Skiing Area	Swamp

CONVERSION TABLES

°C = (°F - 32) / 1.8
°F = (°C x 1.8) + 32
1 inch = 2.54 centimeters (cm)
1 foot = 0.304 meters (m)
1 yard = 0.914 meters
1 mile = 1.6093 kilometers (km)
1 km = 0.6214 miles
1 fathom = 1.8288 m
1 chain = 20.1168 m
1 furlong = 201.168 m
1 acre = 0.4047 hectares
1 sq km = 100 hectares
1 sq mile = 2.59 square km
1 ounce = 28.35 grams
1 pound = 0.4536 kilograms
1 short ton = 0.90718 metric ton
1 short ton = 2,000 pounds
1 long ton = 1.016 metric tons
1 long ton = 2,240 pounds
1 metric ton = 1,000 kilograms
1 quart = 0.94635 liters
1 US gallon = 3.7854 liters
1 Imperial gallon = 4.5459 liters
1 nautical mile = 1.852 km

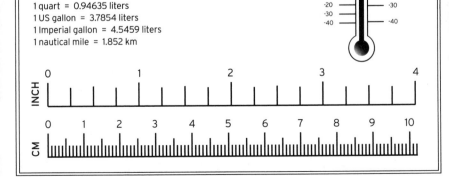

MOON SAN JUAN &
PUERTO RICO'S EAST COAST
Avalon Travel
a member of the Perseus Books Group
1700 Fourth Street
Berkeley, CA 94710, USA
www.moon.com

Editor and Series Manager: Kathryn Ettinger
Copy Editor: Christopher Church
Graphics Coordinators: Sean Bellows,
    Kathryn Osgood
Production Coordinators: Sean Bellows,
    Domini Dragoone, Elizabeth Jang
Cover Designer: Kathryn Osgood
Map Editor: Brice Ticen
Cartographer: Kat Bennett
Proofreader: Julie Littman

ISBN-13: 978-1-59880-387-7

Some photos and illustrations are used by permission
and are the property of the original copyright
owners.

Front cover photo: Guard Tower at Fort San
Cristobal, San Juan © dreamstime.com
Title page photo: Old San Juan, the original capital
of Puerto Rico © JEDphoto / 123rf.com

Printed in the United States by Edwards Brothers

ABOUT THE AUTHOR

Suzanne Van Atten

Experienced editor and travel writer Suzanne Van Atten has written about destinations throughout the United States, Mexico, South America, the Caribbean, and Europe. She has snorkeled a shipwreck in Aruba, gone ballroom dancing in Rio de Janeiro, barhopped in Barcelona, slept in a Jesuit monastery on the Amalfi coast, crewed a hot air balloon in New Mexico, gone white-water rafting in Tennessee, and gotten lost too many times to count. Suzanne is currently an editor for the *Atlanta Journal-Constitution*.

Amidst all these travels, the one place she always returns to is Puerto Rico, a place she fell in love with when she lived there for two years as a teenager. The rich Spanish culture, postcard-perfect beaches, lush tropical jungle, cobblestone streets, pastel colors, lively music, and the joie de vivre of its people colluded to seduce her. No matter how many times she returns, she always discovers something new and delightful to keep her coming back.